TABLE OF CONTENTS

ABOUT THE BOOK

This book is intended to be a resource for individuals in the retirement transition — specifically, individuals who have had a rewarding career but are nonetheless facing retirement, either by choice or by circumstance. Having spent several years talking with many retirees (and pre-retirees) about their experiences, and sorting through hundreds of scientific studies, I uncovered various personal and emotional changes that individuals experience in the retirement transition. Additionally, I found retirees often relied on common strategies for successfully navigating life changes in retirement. Based on this work, my intention is for this book to help raise awareness with regard to personal life changes, and ease the retirement transition for those who might otherwise find it difficult.

With a background in Industrial-Organizational Psychology, I also believe that many of the ideas and knowledge generated in this field may be applicable in retirement as well. It is widely accepted that differences in personality and motivation, as well as situational factors will impact our job satisfaction. Retirement advice typically does not take into consideration individual preferences, motivation, and circumstances. For instance, retirees are often advised to volunteer and join social groups; however, such activities may not always be the right fit. Those who tend to be more extraverted may thrive in a retirement that involves frequent contact with many different people. Introverts, on the other hand, may not want to spend all of their time in volunteer or other social groups; instead, they may gain more satisfaction from focusing on a few close relationships.

Retirement is therefore described here as a unique, individual experience.

While this book is written for a general audience, with some general recommendations, the reader is also guided through a reflective process, which takes into account personal circumstances and preferences. Retirement is therefore described here as a unique, individual experience—just as each individual's career is unique. Retirement is a life chapter, which is yours to design.

Most people adjust well to retirement. However, researchers find that anywhere from 10% to 30% tend to struggle with the transition.[1] A larger number may still go through a period of adjustment, though less difficult. I have found many retirees, who are satisfied and well-adjusted, still report experiencing significant life adjustments. In an extensive review of research, I uncovered various adjustments and challenges reported by retirees. These adjustments and challenges are not reflective of everyone's experience with retirement, nor are they meant to illustrate retirement as an inherently difficult process. Rather, they reflect various areas where retirement may involve life changes and adjustments. Additionally, strategies that supported a smooth transition to retirement were identified in this research, which may be of benefit to others in the transition. These issues and strategies form the basis of the sections included in this book: *Retirement as a Process, Who You Are, What You Do, Who Is Involved,* and *How You Structure It.*

Case studies are also included throughout this book, based on work with retirees in both the U.K. and the U.S. (pseudonyms have been used to protect identity). Many of these stories offer real-life examples of the points discussed. Some interviewees had completed the retirement transition and were looking back at their journey; others were still making adjustments to a new way of life, or still in the pre-retirement phase, and could therefore offer insights as to how they felt at a particular point in time.

It may also be useful to outline what this book is not intended for: as suggested in the title, this book does not address financial matters. There are other resources and professionals that may help in this area, as it does form the foundation for retirement. If finances are a big concern for you, it is advisable to seek guidance on those matters before proceeding to other aspects of retirement. However, just like factors beyond compensation have been found to have a profound impact on wellbeing at work, this book is focused on such non-financial factors that contribute to wellbeing in retirement.

Similarly, this book does not directly address physical health - apart from a short discussion of beliefs about the impact of retirement on health. Again there are many other resources and professionals available for support in terms of physical health. As with finances, health also plays a significant role in general satisfaction and wellbeing. But, again, there are many factors beyond these that may play an important role in retirement adjustment and general wellbeing. Additionally, some of these factors may serve to improve physical health. For instance, as we'll discuss later on, some researchers have found that social group memberships, in retirement, have a positive effect on physical health – an effect comparable to that of physical exercise.[2]

This book is also not intended to be about volunteering, keeping busy, or other suggestions as to how you should spend your time in retirement. Rather, it looks at changes that are commonly experienced, as well as fundamental factors underlying wellbeing in both work and retirement. More importantly, it includes strategies for successfully managing changes and a reflective process to help you explore how these factors apply to your personal circumstances. It is also not about developing a rigid plan that you must follow to a tee; it is intended to plant seeds for you to consider as you make your own journey, and may come across experiences similar to those described here.

Lastly, to one of the premises of this book, retirement varies from person to person. As such, most people will find that some of these sections are more relevant to their own retirement situation than others. For instance, you may find that the social side of the transition is more important to you than identity-related changes, or vice versa. Some of you may also find that you transition to retirement without any difficulties, while others may go through a natural phase of disappointment or letdown before discovering a satisfying new lifestyle.

PATHWAYS TO RETIREMENT: CASE STUDIES

A TEACHER'S UNFOUNDED FEAR OF RETIREMENT

When Janet looked in the mirror in the mornings before work, she saw a teacher. It was a comfortable identity that played a huge part in making her life whole and satisfying, despite the stress and increasing demands being placed on teachers. She never really thought about the end of her career, until her husband accepted an early retirement package. She knew in the back of her mind that her role would end one day, but it came around far sooner than she expected. The plan, when they had both retired, was to move from South Carolina to Reno, Nevada - to be near their children and grandchildren. Janet was in full agreement with this, and looked forward to a new life out west, so all that remained was for her to leave her job. However, the inevitability of leaving behind her identity, her home and her friends was like a dark cloud of fear and uncertainty following her around as she approached her own retirement.

Three years into retirement, Janet and her husband are well into a new phase of life in Reno. After the initial adjustment of a cross-country move, she and her husband quickly involved themselves in local activities, making mutual friends. They also made sure they retained a degree of independence from one another by pursuing individual activities. Today they lead an active, outdoor lifestyle with hiking, cycling, and kayaking. Janet also recently started a personal project, writing memoirs of her mother's experiences during World War II. For Janet, this project is a source of meaning, combining use of her writing skills with an exploration of her family history. None of this negates the importance of her past life as a teacher; that will always remain a vital part of her life story. But allowing that phase to come to its natural end opened up the opportunities for a new phase of life, and an expansion of her identity in ways that she had not imagined before.

FROM A DEDICATED LEADER TO A VOLUNTEER AND FAMILY MAN

Andrew spent 31 years working 12-14 hour days, including weekends, and traveling extensively for a global technology company. Throughout these years, he was proud of the positive and substantial changes he was able to make within the company. An even greater source of satisfaction was working with his colleagues around the world, finding ways to motivate teams to work more effectively and efficiently together. This came at a cost, however: he had sacrificed considerable time with his family, and missed much of his children growing up. At age 58, Andrew felt that it was time to try to address this, and to begin focusing on his family and personal life before it was too late. He still had the relative youth and stamina to work, and for a time considered trying to find another full time job. However the more he thought about it, the more he was drawn to undertaking volunteer work instead.

The transition to this new lifestyle was not easy. After a honeymoon phase in the early part of retirement, Andrew struggled with a bit of malaise and even some feelings of depression. Despite being a generally ambitious and goal-oriented person, he often found himself doing nothing. There were so many things he wanted to do. However, on many days he found himself looking at his watch and realizing it was already 4pm. The day had nearly passed, and he hadn't yet done any of the things he'd planned to.

It was then that Andrew realized he needed to get involved with some non-profit organizations and create more of a structure and routine with his free time. This commitment would give him both a sense of structure and a sense of purpose for the day. At the same time, it would still be flexible enough for him to adjust his schedule as he wished.

Today, ten years after his retirement, Andrew enjoys a comfortable balance between travel with his wife, projects around the house, pursuits in aviation, and involvement with several non-profits, both religious and business oriented. In addition to providing some structure to his days, his involvement with these organizations allows him to utilize his knowledge and years of experience, and also continue to work with people. However, he also appreciates the importance of balancing his voluntary commitments with other hobbies and, of course, his family.

A BUSY EXECUTIVE'S UNPLANNED TRANSITION TO A WORKING RETIREMENT

Bill is the kind of guy who is always on the move, he has trouble sitting still for long. During his teenage years, this energy was directed toward his interest in cars, theater, and art. His family was not supportive of these pursuits for a career path, however, and nudged him toward a more professional career, which in the end became one as a business analyst.

Bill's restless energy resulted in success both as a business analyst at a top-consulting firm and as a turn-around CEO. Career and work were central to his life: from social events to sitting on boards and committees, his daily activities mostly revolved around his job. As a result, the prospect of retiring was a very daunting one - like going 'from 60 to 0 in about 2 seconds.' Retirement was inevitable, however, and he planned on doing so by leaving a company he had been with for the last eight years. After completing his work to turn the company around, he had been asked to continue as CEO. However, he now he felt the company would be in good hands without his involvement. So he identified and trained a successor; and when he was convinced that the successor was ready, he retired.

Bill had given little thought as to what retirement really meant. The first step was to load up his car and move from Kansas to central Texas to be with his partner, who was quite busy and active with her own career. Once there, he wasn't sure what he would do. His partner advised him to say yes to every invitation or opportunity during the first year and then keep what he enjoyed doing and weed out the things he didn't. He followed this advice and his time quickly filled up with requests to help with various volunteer efforts, several of which he had little or no interest in. Eventually, he found himself going back to old interests in art and theater. Then, through referrals, he began re-entering the business world.

Four years after retirement he is as busy as ever, running a business with his partner, volunteering on committees, participating in the local theater, and pursuing his interest in art. Retirement mission accomplished: his restless energy had been redirected from a singular focus on career, to multiple areas of interest.

Retirement for Bill, as it is for many people, was a leap into the unknown. It seemed to be a complete 180 from everything he had been doing, and who he was. But he made the leap his own, creating his own form of retirement. As a result, he has found a combination of activities that reflect the person he is: his lively personality, his drive to always add value, and his lifelong interest in arts.

AN EVOLVING IDENTITY FOR A DISTINGUISHED PROFESSOR

At 66, John retired from his distinguished career as a Scientist and Professor. From a poor upbringing, he went on to publish over 200 articles in peer-reviewed journals, win numerous awards, and gain recognition as a leading expert in his field. After 36 years, he felt he had accomplished enough. Retirement was a personal choice for him; nonetheless, the decision came with many reservations and anxiety about the unknown. With a solid financial plan in place, his concerns revolved around his personal drive, enjoyment of work, and, perhaps most of all, his identification with work. With work being such a big part of his life, retirement was a great abyss of uncertainty.

He also had concerns about no longer earning an income. He had worked hard throughout his career to become financially secure, and avoid ever going back to the poverty-stricken life he experienced as a child. Because of his avid focus on saving, and the somewhat modest lifestyle he had lived, he was better financially prepared than most. Nonetheless, the inherent fear of leaving behind paid employment, and possibly experiencing poverty again, remained.

Despite his fears, John made the leap into the unknown. It was not a gradual transition. He went from a busy semester - teaching and completing research projects - to packing up and closing the door of his office. In one day, he went from a well-respected professor, to a retiree. He was totally unsure of what this next chapter in life would hold; he regarded the future with an odd mixture of interest, anticipation, and anxiety. As the big day approached, he remained in a state of denial, even up to the last hour. On his last day of work, any pretence that this was just another normal working day evaporated, and he departed his office in a state of something resembling shock. He walked through campus in a daze, passing young students and colleagues on the way.

This sense of shock reappeared throughout the first few months of retirement, but over time it eased, and was replaced with thoughts relating to future plans and to his new and evolving identity. Much of this evolution occurred in a state of solitude, which he generally preferred. John's children had moved away years ago; he kept in contact with them through phone calls and occasional visits. John liked where he lived and had no plans to move to be near them, which would have proven difficult as they traveled for work quite a bit. His girlfriend also lived two hours away and was still working, which meant weekend visits.

After nearly three years, John has adjusted well to retirement. He found that he did not miss the identity of being a Professor so much, and he found the all-important flow* with a bit of follow-up consulting work on a former research project, as well as gardening and fiction writing. He has time to pursue other personal interests such as history and astronomy, and he also spends more time doing physical activities now that he's not working. He switches between cross-country skiing, bike riding, hiking, and gardening around his acre of land, depending on the season. He also maintains confidence in his financial situation through regular visits with his financial advisor, to discuss any changes he may need to make. Retirement has evolved from a dark abyss to a comfortable phase of life, free of the politics, strife, and the stresses of work.

*Flow is a psychological state in which you become completely immersed and absorbed by what you are doing[1]

INTRODUCTION

There are many preconceptions, and perhaps misconceptions, around retirement. These could include the assumption that retirement is like going on vacation, where you happily fill your time with travel, an old hobby, or just enjoy doing nothing. Many people count down the days to their retirement. Generally, retirement is seen as a privilege, a luxury even. Others will probably see you as lucky and envy your newfound freedom.

For those not ready to retire, it might feel more like a curse than a privilege. There may appear to be little opportunity for reward and fulfillment in retirement, particularly for those who received a great deal of satisfaction from work. In the extreme, retirement may be seen as 'the end' – a prelude to uselessness, poor health, or even death. Clearly, such beliefs will lead some to avoid retirement.

However, neither of these extremes represents reality for most retirees. Retirement is often a more moderate transition, with ups and downs, and pros and cons, just as with other life transitions. The decision to retire may involve a mix of emotions - excitement and uncertainty, hope and fear, regret and gladness. It can be a confusing mix of both benefits and losses. While you may have some negative thoughts about retirement, the idea of managing your own time, as you wish, is probably appealing. Even those who look to continue work, in some form, tend to opt for more flexible work arrangements in order to free up some of their time. Or, you may really enjoy your work, but other factors are pushing you to retire.

For some people, the opportunity to fully consider how and when to retire may not arise: retirement may be enforced, or occur early due to circumstances beyond control. Health issues, caregiving responsibilities, and employment circumstances are the cause of sooner than planned retirements for as many as 60% of retirees in the US.[1] These individuals do not have the luxury of mixed emotions in making the decision to retire. Retirement, for them, may be more a process of coming to terms with the inevitable loss of work and, effectively, being retired.[2]

Whether or not retirement is a matter of personal choice, it tends to involve substantial life changes and personal adjustments. There is likely to be considerable change in how you spend your time and organize your day. It will also mean a shift in identity – how you see yourself and how others see you. Furthermore, it is not only an individual transition; it is one that often impacts our relationships with others, including colleagues, friends, and spouses. So while we tend to think of retirement as something that simply happens overnight, for many people it is more of a process, adjusting to these changes before settling into this new chapter of life. With planning and preparation, of course, these changes are less likely to become major disruptions.

Improvements in technology and healthcare are also increasing longevity, and transforming retirement. In Europe and North America, most people retiring at 65 can expect to live another 18-20 years, much of which will be spent active and healthy.[3] This makes for a very different retirement from that experienced by earlier generations: one that now represents a longer and more active phase of life.

Retirement planning still focuses almost solely on finances; and with a longer retirement, there is a need for long-term planning and more savings. However, there is also a need to consider what this next chapter in life will entail. Employers are beginning to offer more well-rounded retirement courses, with attention to life changes. Generally, however, this area tends to be overlooked or only briefly discussed. With as many as one in three people struggling with the transition, it is an area worthy of much greater attention.[4]

This book is therefore designed to be a general resource for those transitioning to retirement or recently retired. It provides a framework for designing this next chapter of your life and for making a smooth transition as you navigate changes in day-to-day life. A key aim is to address some of the many personal, non-financial adjustments commonly encountered in this transition, and to highlight strategies that have helped others adapt to a new life without both the burdens and benefits of work. The intention is not to create a prescriptive guide for how to approach retirement, but rather to bring to attention the changes and challenges commonly encountered. It also provides a framework for designing a satisfying new lifestyle, aligned with your priorities and preferences.

Each chapter of this book introduces key factors that have appeared to play an important role in the retirement transition, as established through fieldwork and research. The first two sections, *The Beginning: Your Career* and *Your Retirement Vision*, explore the context of your retirement, by considering your personal story and retirement vision. This is the launch pad for your retirement, and is worth reviewing whether you are contemplating retirement or already retired. *Retirement as a Process* addresses the process of adjustment, and different phases commonly encountered in the transition. The subsequent sections highlight what are considered to be the four key components of life in retirement:

- *Who You Are* explores changes to identity and the central role this plays in designing a new lifestyle.
- *What You Do* highlights one of the most common questions surrounding retirement— how will you spend your time?
- *Who Is Involved* gives consideration to your social connections and close personal relationships, including spousal relationships.
- *How You Structure It* examines the re-organization of daily life in retirement and the potential impact of having an abundance of free time.

Retirement experiences vary considerably from person to person and, because of this, some sections may resonate with you more than others. You may find that some of the factors discussed in this book evolve quite naturally, and demand little attention, while other factors may play a more significant part in the transition. With a series of reflective questions in each section, the book will help you identify how these factors are relevant to your own retirement, and explore the lifestyle and activities that will contribute to personal fulfillment. Making notes on each section of reflective questions is advisable, and will create useful reference points as you progress through the book or to return to at a later stage.

BACKGROUND PERSPECTIVES ON RETIREMENT

Retirement is a relatively new concept; originally coming to life with the establishment of social security in Germany in 1889.[5] The United Kingdom and United States followed suit with state pension in 1909, and social security in 1935. However, with benefits starting between 65 and 70 years, and life expectancy around 50 to 55 years, few people enjoyed retirement as we tend to think of it today. Those who did receive benefits were likely struggling with poor health and inability to continue paid work – hence the reason for establishing such benefits in the first place.

Today, we expect to enjoy a fairly lengthy retirement, with good health, and receiving benefits from the system we paid into. With benefits still being offered between approximately 60 and 70 years, life expectancy in the 80's, and major improvements in healthcare, retirement has become a new chapter in life – one that is longer and more active than for earlier generations. As with the start of a new career, people are now asking themselves how they want to spend this chapter of their life.

Some argue that the word retirement should be retired, suggesting it is no longer applicable as people are either choosing or being forced to continue work.[6] On the other hand, retirement is still something discussed and planned for as sort of an end game for one's career. Commercials also portray ideals of travel, leisure, and consumption in retirement. Many people are also pushed to retire despite expectations to continue working.[7] So the reality is that retirement continues to be a relevant life chapter for many people, although the nature of retirement is changing. There seems to be a tendency toward continuing paid work in some form. Motivations for continuing work are both the financial benefit and the interest in continuing meaningful work.[8] While people may argue over how we define retirement, some consider a bit of paid work to be part of their personal vision for retirement. In other words, some people retire from their careers, and then continue to enjoy some form of paid work, but still consider themselves to be retired. This is something to keep in mind as you develop your personal vision for retirement; would it involve some paid work?

Academic perspectives on retirement have also shifted. Early research portrayed it as a negative event, involving stress, challenges, and poor health and wellbeing.[9] More recently, retirement has been portrayed in a positive light by researchers. However, the dominant view now emerging is that retirement is a complex process, with varied trajectories and outcomes.[10] There are not only differences between individuals' experiences of retirement, but each person's experience may change over time (see section on *Retirement as a Process*). Numerous factors, from individual characteristics to employment circumstances and societal trends have an impact on these varied experiences. The bottom line is that it is better not to generalize with regard to the retirement transition; it is very much an individual experience shaped by unique circumstances.

CHANGES IN HEALTH AND WELLBEING AFTER RETIREMENT

How does retirement impact health and wellbeing? One of the goals of this book and other resources on retirement preparation is to reduce the potentially negative impact of retirement. Talking with people about retirement, you will certainly hear anecdotal evidence of the detrimental effects it seems to have on once healthy and ambitious individuals. As was discussed at the beginning of this chapter, however, most people will experience a more moderate transition to retirement, with both benefits and losses. For instance, many retirees enjoy spending more time with family, but also miss their interactions with coworkers. Others might miss the challenge work provided, but find they are less stressed and actually healthier in retirement.

Again, there are also significant differences in individuals' experiences of retirement. Researchers from two separate studies examined changes in wellbeing over the course of the retirement transition; from pre-retirement to several years after retirement.[11] They found significant differences between individuals, with various patterns of adjustment. For instance, Dr. Mo Wang with Portland State University found that the majority of retirees (approximately 70%) experienced minimal changes in wellbeing after retirement; another group of retirees (approximately 20%) experienced a temporary decline in wellbeing. Finally, approximately 5% of retirees experienced a slight and steady increase in wellbeing - these retirees tended to have low job satisfaction in their prior employment, and tended to retire from highly physically demanding or highly stressful jobs.

In summary, retirement itself does not appear to have a generally positive or negative impact; rather, circumstances and individual characteristics contribute to very different experiences with it. Furthermore, retirement is a process that may involve changes in wellbeing while one adjusts to a new lifestyle. Those that find it difficult early on will often adjust and experience a subsequent recovery in wellbeing. Alternatively, those that experience an increase in wellbeing during a honeymoon stage of retirement may find this tapers off as they settle in. Finally, others may experience retirement with more continuity, and little change in wellbeing.

DOES RETIREMENT HAVE AN IMPACT ON PHYSICAL HEALTH?

It is often suggested that retirement leads to poor health. Some articles in popular media might scare you right back into the idea of working forever. However, research in this area has produced conflicting results – some studies report negative effects of retirement on health while others report positive effects.[12] It does appear, however, that recent studies are finding that retirement has more positive effects on health.[13] Those retiring from highly stressful or physically demanding jobs may see the most significant, positive impact on health after retirement. Others also find that it has a positive impact on their health, allowing more time for exercise and cooking healthy meals. On the other hand, those who become less physically active in retirement may experience declining health.

Along the same lines as the misconception that retirement leads to poor health is a tendency to equate retirement with old age. There is a negative attitude toward retirement that is rooted in negative beliefs about aging (ageism). Rather than celebrating and respecting elders, western cultures emphasize youthfulness and health, with the ability to actively participate in paid work. Ageism has a broad impact, from an engagement in cosmetic procedures to difficulties finding employment.[14] Wisdom, life experience, and other virtues of old age are largely overlooked. Interestingly, many people entering old age still hold onto some of these culturally formed stereotypes about aging.[15] In essence, we are stereotyping our future selves (or current selves). The result is an active resistance to indicators of old age, again, through things like cosmetic surgery, and also, it seems, by resisting retirement.

The impact of these negative attitudes toward retirement and aging appears to a big one – leading to reduced longevity.[16] Researchers in one study found that those with positive attitudes toward aging lived, on average, 7.5 years longer than those with negative attitudes toward aging.[17] To some extent, it seems people's beliefs about aging and retirement contributed to a self-fulfilling prophecy that resulted in a shorter lifespan. This may happen as beliefs guide our actions, which may or may not support health and longevity.

THE BEGINNING: YOUR CAREER

Nearing retirement, Bob reflected back on his career. It was not intended to be a predictable progression to upper management, although that may appear to have happened in hindsight. He started with a degree in public policy, after which he found a comfortable position with the local government. He enjoyed his work, but it did not run his life. His managers, however, recognized his diplomatic abilities and quickly identified him as a potential leader. Years later, he found himself succeeding the CEO of this local government organization. He has now been in this position for 10 years, enjoying the exposure to many different groups of people, the constant problem solving, and the opportunity to utilize his skills in diplomacy. He is now approaching retirement age, and while he has a sound financial plan, he has only a vague idea of what his retirement will hold.

As historian, James Burke, is famously quoted as saying 'you can only know where you're going if you know where you've been'. With all the time you spent in your career, it is worth taking some time to acknowledge what that involved, what you accomplished, and what you learned along the way. After all, this serves as the prelude to your retirement story. Perhaps there are things you will be happy to let go of, other things you're reluctant to leave behind, and finally some things that will remain part of your life and who you are as an individual.

William Bridges refers to the *endings phase* of life transitions as a closing of one chapter before beginning the next.[1] It is about honoring and letting go of those things that are coming to an end, allowing yourself to move on to whatever is next. In terms of your retirement transition, a reflection on your career allows you to explore the aspects of work that have been the most rewarding and enjoyable. These may be the things you will need to come to terms with leaving behind; or, perhaps finding a way to continue in some way. Acknowledging these endings, before your actual retirement, may prevent any negativity around this from taking you by surprise later on.

Alternatively, more negative aspects of work may be quite easy to leave behind, and point to the benefits of retirement.

REFLECTIVE QUESTIONS

Tell the story of your career.
What stands out in terms of accomplishments or milestones, challenges you overcame, and lessons you learned?

Reflecting over the course of your career, what were the most satisfying moments?
What was it about these points in your career that you found satisfying?

YOUR RETIREMENT VISION

With grown-up children having left home, and the arrival of several grandchildren, Cassandra is ready to retire from a successful career in real estate. She has always loved her work but is ready to leave the rat race and city traffic behind. While she adores her grandchildren, her vision for retirement is one of slowing down, smelling the roses, and focusing on herself. She plans to spend quality time with her grandchildren of course, but she is not interested in a life that revolves solely around them. Instead, she will focus on her own personal interests and goals, one of them being travel.

Everyone has a different vision for retirement - whether it involves continuing some form of work, more time with family, slowing down to appreciate life, or more time for personal pursuits. Retirement comes in all shapes and sizes, and no one lifestyle will suit everyone.

As you approach retirement, others may begin offering advice on how to spend your time in retirement. However, it is important to step back and reflect on your own vision for this next chapter in life, perhaps with the same consideration as you most likely gave to your career. What does retirement mean to you? Ideally, how would you like to spend your time? How can you make this a reality? Advice from others, including from this book, may then help you further refine this personal vision.

REFLECTIVE QUESTIONS

What does retirement mean to you?
Ideally, how would you like to spend your time? Then think about how could you realistically make this happen.

Imagine what an ideal day might look like in retirement. How would the day go? What would you be doing? What is it about this day that would be ideal?

Practice visualizing yourself in retirement: Visualisation techniques have been found to be highly effective in goal achievement; they even work to rewire neural pathways in our brain, perhaps guiding our behavior toward actions in line with our goals – but that's a topic for another book.[1] For now, take a moment to simply close your eyes and imagine yourself, ideally, at some point in your retirement. If you have concerns about retirement, now is a time to put those aside and focus on a positive, personalized vision for retirement. Reflect on a particular day and again, ideally, what you are doing, what you see, who you are with, and perhaps most importantly, how you feel. Take a moment to simply explore and embrace this image.

RETIREMENT AS A PROCESS: PHASES AND STAGES

Retirement is not merely the cessation of work, or a change of job status, that happens over night. It is a significant departure from the working life you have grown accustomed to. It is a new phase of life that can last upwards of 20 years; one in which your day-to-day life is no longer defined by work. It may therefore also involve a personal and emotional process of adjusting to these major life changes. While some seem to settle right into retirement, others find it takes a bit of time, exploration, and even some trial and error before settling into a satisfying new lifestyle.

Retirement as a process may actually start several years before you leave work, with the planning, anticipation, and finally the decision to retire. Some people are also mentally preparing themselves for this change with shifting values and priorities, well before they get there. The retirement event itself, when you actually leave full-time work, is also a significant and sometimes emotional part of the process. After this, you may experience a honeymoon phase where you enjoy time to relax and unwind, travel, or do things you did not have time to do before.[1] You could also, however, experience a period of disappointment or letdown, as the novelty of retirement and your newfound freedom wear off. At this point, many people will make some adjustments to their routine or activities, and subsequently settle into a more long-term, satisfying lifestyle.

The following sections examine significant points or phases in the process of retirement. As Robert Atchley emphasized in his work on stages of retirement, not everyone will experience all of these phases; and each phase may be experienced quite differently from person to person.[1] For instance, the retirement event may be an abrupt ending of full-time work and beginning of full-retirement. Or, it may be more of a gradual transition to part-time or occasional work. It may be a time of celebration and excitement or a time of shock and uncertainty. Despite the differences, these phases highlight the way in which retirement experiences may fluctuate over time, involving different emotions, and calling for new changes.

THE RETIREMENT DECISION

The retirement decision became a pressing issue for Phil after a meeting with his financial advisor. He was informed that, with the pension and benefits he would receive upon his 65th birthday, continuing work past this point would be of little to no financial benefit. Phil very much enjoyed his work, so it was only then that he began seriously thinking about retirement.

Upon further reflection and a few changes at work, Phil's retirement decision became more than a financial matter. Firstly, another leader in his organization announced his impending retirement, before Phil had a chance to announce his own plans. Secondly, the organization faced a directive to begin downsizing. As CEO, Phil was personally invested in the successful operation of this organization and felt that his retirement in the midst of these events would be too disruptive. He also began to wonder what his retirement would be like while his wife was still heading off to work each morning. She enjoyed her work and was not planning to retire just yet; but he had not really considered how he would spend his time before she would finally retire.

Phil still planned to retire; however, he needed to adjust the timing of his departure to align with his values and commitment to the organization. He also had some thinking to do about the initial part of his retirement, before his wife retired.

The retirement decision is all too often solely attributed to an individual's financial situation. In reality, however, other factors usually play a highly important role, such as work and career circumstances, personal preferences, health, or family needs. We also tend to assume that we will have control over the timing of retirement; yet, it is often more a matter of circumstances than personal choice. For those thinking they will "never retire," it may therefore be wise to at least consider a plan B, if circumstances push them to retire. Whichever the case, there are common factors that will push or pull you toward retirement, or toward continuing work, including[2]:

- **Health**, next to finances, is often a primary consideration in the retirement decision. Poor health forces some into retirement, while others wish to retire while they still have their health and the ability to enjoy an active lifestyle. Those in stressful or physically demanding jobs may also retire in order to improve their health, and do tend to experience this benefit.

- **Family and personal responsibilitie**s are another common reason for considering retirement versus continued employment. Providing financial support to others may require continued work while family caregiving needs often push people to retire.

- **Employment circumstances** (e.g., redundancies, cut-backs, or new leadership) also tend to play a central role in the retirement decision, often pushing an individual to retire before they are ready. Additionally, many people find that changes in the workplace make it less desirable for them to continue working. On the other hand, some find that their loyalty and commitment to others is preventing them from retiring. In this case, it may help to begin developing an exit strategy that will ensure others are still supported as you transition to retirement.

- **Personal goals** will of course drive the retirement decision, assuming it is your choice, as well as how you decide to spend your retirement. For instance, many people today are choosing to pursue new careers as part of their retirement. However, you may also feel that you have accomplished enough in your career and you are ready to move on to other things.

- **Lifestyle preferences** are a central part of financial planning for retirement – advisors will examine your lifestyle, or suggest adjustments to your lifestyle, when assessing how much money you will need and when you can comfortably retire. For many people, retirement means a reduction in income, and therefore adjusting one's lifestyle.

- **Retirement attitudes and expectations** also tend to steer individuals rather strongly either toward or away from retirement. Do you view retirement as freedom and opportunity, or as old age? Do you have fears about retirement that prevent you from considering it? Viewing retirement as old age tends to be associated with continued work, of course. Equating retirement with old age is not usually an accurate or complete picture of retirement; furthermore, negative stereotypes of old age have been found to have a negative impact on adjustment and even longevity.[3] As we explore throughout this book, retirement is much more than a time of old age – it is an entirely new opportunity, and often lengthy life chapter.

- **Opportunities for paid work in retirement** might make the decision to transition fairly easy, making it a gradual transition where you may enjoy a bit of both worlds.

- **Job satisfaction** may also play into your retirement decision. Many people choose to retire even when they have really enjoyed their work. However, dissatisfaction with work will most likely lead one to retire, when the opportunity presents itself.

REFLECTIVE QUESTIONS

Personal decisions are often aided by considering pros and cons in possible scenarios. Here we'll consider factors that may be pushing or pulling you toward retirement, or toward continued work.

What factors are pulling you toward retirement – i.e., factors that make retirement attractive to you?

What factors are *pushing* you to consider retirement – i.e., circumstances that make retirement likely?

What factors are pulling you toward continuing work – i.e., factors you find attractive about continuing work?

What factors are pushing you toward continuing work – i.e., circumstances making you feel like you *should* continue work?

THE UNKNOWN: UNCERTAINTY IN THE TRANSITION TO RETIREMENT

Will I enjoy retirement, or will I miss work? Will my money last? Will I maintain good health? These are some of the uncertainties on the minds of those approaching retirement. Whether or not one's retirement is planned, uncertainty is often a cause of stress and anxiety in the approach to retirement. It seems to be an inherent part of the retirement transition, as with other transitions in life.

The extent to which uncertainty troubles you, or causes stress, will depend not only on your ability to plan or predict, but on your tolerance for uncertainty – some thrive in ambiguous and uncertain situations while others prefer more predictability.[4] You may also rely on particular strategies for coping with uncertainty. Below are some effective strategies for coping with uncertainty, in general, as well as more specific strategies for coping with financial uncertainty (of course, the more general strategies also apply to financial uncertainty). The first and most important strategy is one you are already employing by reading this book – planning and preparation.

Planning and preparation

Anxiety about uncertain situations often leads people to avoid talking about, and thinking about, those situations. This may be the reason many people fail to prepare financially for retirement: because it causes anxiety. Unfortunately, this avoidance may only serve to exacerbate the problem. So the first and most important step to dealing with uncertainty is to start preparing – just as you are now preparing for the non-financial side of retirement. Even if you are already retired, you may find that preparing, for what is still to come, may help reduce the anxiety associated with unknowns.

Focus on what you can control

Psychologist Robert Leahy differentiates between productive and unproductive worry.[5] Fretting over things you cannot control is unproductive worry. Productive worry, on the other hand, refers to worry about the things that are within your immediate control, at least to some degree. It means focusing on the things you can take action on, say, in the next 24 hours. Arranging to meet with a financial advisor, for instance, is an actionable step you can take in the next 24 hours. Reading this book and other resources on retirement is another example of an actionable step for those who are feeling uncertain about life in retirement. If you are a chronic worrier, Robert Leahy's book *The Worry Cure* will provide more valuable tips to address other forms of worry.

Creating some structure and predictability

We will sometimes react to uncertainty by *creating* certainty and predictability, or, imposing it on an uncertain situation. We might do this by trying to set a clear course of action or make concrete plans. However, while this may help to reduce feelings of uncertainty, at least temporarily, it may also blind us to new opportunities, or to the need to adapt and change directions. It is therefore advisable to do this by developing short-term goals with flexible plans. In the early part of retirement, this may involve having some planned activities and a bit of routine, but not so much that you have no room for exploration.

Utilize healthy stress reduction techniques

Excessive drinking is an increasing problem with retirees.[6] For most people it seems to be harmless fun; but it can of course become problematic. Drinking can be an unhealthy coping mechanism in the face of uncertainty and stress, along with things like gambling or compulsive spending. These usually make things worse, creating further stress. Activities such as yoga, meditation, walking, or other forms exercise are examples of healthier stress reduction techniques. They also have the added benefit of improving physical health.

Recognizing opportunities in uncertain transitions

Part of coping with uncertainty means simply accepting that there will be some uncertainty, and perhaps recognizing the benefits it may afford. It is often in messy, in-between phases of life that new possibilities may arise.[7] Without overly structured routines and obligations, you may see opportunities you would not see otherwise. So, as is discussed later in this chapter (see *Exploration, Trial and Error, and Adjustment*), it may also benefit you to simply embrace a bit of ambiguity and allow for some exploration.

Coping with financial uncertainty

Even with a plan in place, there is often a good deal of financial uncertainty in retirement. The question of whether you can afford retirement depends on numerous factors that are largely unpredictable. Things like the current state of the economy are largely out of our control, as individuals. So, what *can* we do in terms of coping with this uncertainty?

- **Take a break from the news.** The news is notorious for being negative; and news of troubled financial times, in particular, is often a source of financial stress. You may enjoy keeping up with current events, but consider limiting your exposure to negative financial news, and notice the difference in how you feel when you do take a break.

- **Step back before making financial decisions.** Our emotions can drive us to want to take immediate action. On the contrary, we may need to slow down and take a step back. Keep in mind that a hurried feeling with purchases is often instigated by sales and marketing techniques. If you notice you are feeling rushed to make a big financial decision, take a moment to step back instead. Gather your thoughts and emotions, and evaluate your reasons before doing anything. If you are dealing with investments or other significant financial decisions, seek counsel from a trusted financial advisor.

- **Focus on non-financial forms of wealth.** Money contributes to happiness, to a certain extent. Once you are able to meet basic needs (e.g., food, shelter, and safety), however, other factors appear to play a more prominent role in wellbeing.[8] Relationships and meaningful pursuits, for instance, are consistently found to be major predictors of happiness and wellbeing.

- **Adjust your mindset towards money.** Although money seems like a fairly objective matter, our fears, beliefs, and attitudes impact our relationship with money. Dr. Sharon Spano explores how mindsets of scarcity and abundance influence our experiences with both time and money, *regardless of how much time or money we actually have.*[9] For instance, Dr. Spano describes people who are always running against the clock, or chasing the dollar. Dr. Brad Klontz and Dr. Ted Klontz have also explored what they call money disorders (e.g., compulsive buying, gambling) and problematic money behaviors, including how they develop and how to beat them.[10]

PLANNING, PREPARATION, AND EXPECTATIONS

Many people count down the days to their retirement, only to find later that *"it wasn't all that it was cracked up to be."* Conversely, others go through months of tremendous anxiety and fear, only to find that they are well suited to life in retirement. In either scenario, unrealistic expectations create unnecessary problems. On the other hand, planning, preparation, and realistic expectations about life in retirement have been found to set the stage for subsequent adjustment and satisfaction.[11] As we discussed in the previous section, they may also help to reduce uncertainty and anxiety.

Many people do not actually give much thought to retirement; that is, until they are nearing retirement, or recently retired and experiencing changes. Because retirement is so different from other phases of life, it is hard to predict how it will feel when you get there. As you are reading this book, you are clearly making an effort to prepare for this change. But what else can you do to prepare? And how do you develop realistic expectations about something so vastly different from the working life you know so well?

First, talk to retirees about their experiences. Ask them what worked well and what didn't work so well for them, while also keeping in mind that people have vastly different experiences with retirement. The range of experiences and opinions will probably become apparent as you speak to different people. Nonetheless, it will give you some ideas, and perhaps some options that resonate with your vision for retirement.

Also, if it's an option, try reducing your hours or taking a sabbatical. This may give you a taste for what retirement will be like. It is still quite different from full-time retirement, over the long haul, but you'll be able to test out some of your ideas for how you might structure the next phase.

Lastly, in order to develop realistic expectations, it's a good idea to challenge your assumptions about retirement. For instance, we talked earlier about the common misconception that retirement leads to poor health. On the contrary, recent research is indicating retirement may have more positive effects on physical health.[12] It usually means less stress, and more time for things like exercise and cooking healthy meals. So consider the stereotypes and associations you make with retirement, and how these may not necessarily reflect your experiences.

Most people find that retirement is not altogether positive or negative. Rather it tends to be a mix of both benefits and losses, having both pros and cons. For instance, you may feel relieved to get away from office politics or stress, but also miss the challenge work provided. Acknowledging that retirement may involve both positive experiences and challenging times is perhaps another step toward setting realistic expectations.

THE RETIREMENT EVENT

Three big recycling bins came and John threw away 40 years worth of journals that no one wanted. He didn't see this as a big deal; he was pretty much in denial about retirement. Then 2:00 came; time to wrap up and get ready for the awards ceremony. He walked across campus like he had hundreds of times, went to the student union and signed in.

The proceedings started with the provost reading his script for each of the emeriti coming up to get their plaques. John's name came up and he got up, shook hands with the president, had his picture taken and sat back down in a daze. Awards were given out for outstanding achievements; he used to receive such awards and, some ten years ago, he received one of those that were bestowed today. He realized how much he enjoyed getting these awards, although he tried hard to hide it. He would miss the validation of his work.

After it was all done, John meandered back to his car and set-off for home. Shock set in again; this was his last real day, other than clearing out his office. By the time he got home, the shock had really gripped him. He turned off the engine of his car and just sat there, unable to move for a while. He knew this day was coming, but it felt so sudden. He had pulled the rug out from under himself and there was no going back.

The day you actually leave full-time work to become 'retired' is a significant, and often emotional, part of the process. The way people experience this ranges from excitement and relief, to holding back tears and feelings of grief. Some may experience a sense of shock, or go into complete denial. Some describe retirement hitting them like a ton of bricks. Others describe feeling like the rug was being pulled out from under them, as John described in the story above. All of these experiences are natural reactions to this significant life event, and are not necessarily reflective of long-term experiences with retirement.

The Gradual Transition

Traditionally, retirement has meant a sudden cessation of paid work – you go from 60 to 0, overnight. However, this is not a desirable way to end a career for many people. Today, there tends to be more of a grey area between work and retirement. Increasingly, people are pursuing more meaningful and more flexible work, rather than transitioning to full-retirement. And they are doing so not only for financial reasons, but also out of personal preference.

A gradual transition through part-time work, or bridge employment (a new role seen as a next step before retirement) offers several benefits. There is the obvious financial benefit. However, it also allows you to ease into retired life. If you are working reduced hours, you might have more time to expand your social network outside of work and explore activities that may become a more central part of your life. It may also allow more time for you and your spouse to adjust to increased time spent together.

Companies are still catching up with the demand for more flexible work options, as well as recruiting older workers. Although over 50's tend to offer a strong work ethic, a great deal of experience, and an interest in meaningful work, many are struggling to find new jobs. So it's important to consider the employment outlook if you are planning to step into something new. Alternatively, you may approach your current employer to negotiate a new role and perhaps more flexible working options.

The Send-off

How your departure from work is marked may also impact how you feel at the time of your retirement. Again, this may be an exciting time for some, or a more difficult time for others. Some describe feeling under-valued or somewhat overlooked if there are no gifts or celebrations offered to signify their retirement. However, even when the occasion is suitably marked by an employer and colleagues, it may fall short of expectations, given the time and energy that has been devoted to work. So, depending on how you are feeling about retirement, a send-off may provide a nice passage, or it may compound the emotional difficulties you face.

Marking your retirement by accepting gifts and parties can be a positive experience and help to bring about acceptance. However, it is worth thinking about what is right for you and your circumstances. Consider the type of celebration you would like to have to signify your retirement, and communicate this to those who will make the arrangements. Think about what, ideally, your last day of work and first day of retirement would look like. You may choose a work party, lunch with co-workers, dinner with family, or you may prefer just to have time to reflect and accept the beginning of a new chapter – you can always organize a get-together with colleagues at a later date when you feel ready. Whatever your send-off looks like, simply beware that it may bring up a bit of emotion as your transition is marked and reality begins to sink in.

REFLECTIVE QUESTIONS

What is your ideal vision for your last day of work? How would you like to see the day proceed?

You might consider who will be there (perhaps for support), what you will be doing, how you will be celebrating, and what you will say to colleagues.

Will you have a celebration for retirement? If so, what will this look like, ideally? Who will be a part of it? Who will help you achieve these visions?

What do you want to say to the colleagues you have worked with, or about the organization you are leaving?

THE INITIAL RETIREMENT EXPERIENCE: HONEYMOON VERSUS DISENCHANTMENT

Just weeks after his retirement, Paul took off with his wife to travel through Arizona, Utah, and New Mexico. This was the beginning of their new adventure, their new life together. No longer tied down by schedules and obligations, Paul was ready to do all the things he hadn't had time for, and travel was a priority.

The travel bug (and healthy retirement savings) took Paul and his wife around the world in the first few years of retirement, visiting Europe, Asia, and even volunteering in remote villages in Africa. Between trips, they caught up with friends, shared their experiences, and worked on projects around the house. It was an exciting and adventurous time, just as he had hoped.

What Paul was not expecting, however, was that even traveling would grow old. Although he was incredibly grateful for the opportunities they had to see the world, something seemed to be missing. He was ready to settle back into life at home, but was not sure what exactly that would look like. Without other retirement plans in mind, he eventually chose to re-enter the workforce, running for a local public office position. His early retirement reflected most people's dreams of retirement; but it was life after this initial excitement that posed challenges. Having not considered what a regular lifestyle would look like in retirement, he simply fell back on what he knew: work.

In the first few days, weeks, and perhaps even months of retirement, you may experience a honeymoon phase - enjoying the freedom and flexibility, time to relax, and time for the things you've always wanted to do.[13] This might include travel, projects around the house, playing golf, or sleeping in and taking it easy. Many people find, however, that the novelty and enjoyment of these things starts to wear off after some time. Activities that were once only enjoyed on the weekends may not be as satisfying when they become an everyday occurrence, as they are no longer a contrast to work. This, of course, can lead to feelings of disappointment, particularly if the enjoyment of such things was part of the plan for retirement.

Some people may skip the honeymoon phase completely, and immediately experience feelings of disappointment and dissatisfaction.[13] This may be more likely to occur when retirement coincides with other life challenges, or when retirement is more a matter of circumstances than personal choice.

For instance, retirement due to poor health may be particularly difficult - involving adjustments both in terms of physical ability and in leaving the workplace.

Either way, these ups and downs are a normal and natural part of the retirement transition. A less than satisfying phase in retirement is not necessarily an indication that you need to return to work, or that you will always feel this way. It may, however, be an indication that you need to make some changes, such as adjusting to relationship changes or finding involvements that contribute to long-term fulfillment – as we'll be discussing in the following chapters.

Retirement Tip: Support networks play a crucial role in the early phase of retirement adjustment. Consider who can offer you support, should you experience some difficulty.

EXPLORATION, TRIAL AND ERROR, AND ADJUSTMENT

After a bit of a honeymoon phase, or perhaps feelings
of disenchantment, you may begin settling into a
new lifestyle. As you do this, however, you may want
to make room for a bit of exploration, testing out
what works for you. Again, it is difficult to know
what retirement will be like until you get there, or
how you will really enjoy spending your time. It can
therefore be very valuable to leave this room for
change, exploration, and trial-and-error.

One of the purposes of this book is to help you
develop clarity and take some time to prepare for
retirement. However, sometimes flexibility is also
key – the space to decide how you feel when you get

there. Don't be afraid to try things out, then gravitate towards the things that are rewarding and away from those that are less so. Part of this experimentation might mean making 'loose' commitments to others, so that you don't feel obligated to continue something you are not enjoying.

> **Retirement Tip:** William Bridges talks about the messy, in-between phase of life transitions, where we explore possibilities and test things out before settling into a new routine. His book, *Transitions: Making Sense of Life's Changes*, is another great resource in preparing for, or adjusting to retirement.

SETTLING INTO RETIREMENT

After these initial highs and lows, and personal adjustments, most people find they settle into a satisfying new lifestyle in retirement. Initial visions of retirement might be replaced by new ways of thinking, or seeking new connections and experiences that hadn't occurred to you before. Alternatively, you may find that living out the retirement you had planned is proving to be rewarding and enjoyable. As we have seen, this is most likely to be the case when you have spent time planning for retirement, or allowed yourself the flexibility to pursue the activities you are drawn to. For those that do experience a bit of a bumpy ride after they retire, it's reassuring to know that with the right mindset, the vast majority of people either continue valued roles and activities or replace work with a rewarding alternative.

Of course, retirement may last many years. So this initial adjustment to retirement is usually not the last 'chapter' or the last transition you will experience. Future circumstances may call for further changes to your lifestyle. Changes in health may require adjustments in your usual set of activities. Alternatively, you may enjoy a slower pace for a while and then decide that you are actually ready for another challenge. Retirement does not have to be the end of the story - you may spend several years on personal pursuits, and then shift your focus to family and vice versa. It's worth keeping an open mind throughout, and revisiting your priorities whenever the time feels right. It may even be helpful to go back to sections in this book and re-evaluate your retirement from time to time – as this is intended as an ongoing reference for your retirement journey.

REFLECTIVE QUESTION

At this point, you may want to revisit your
reflections on your vision for retirement.
What kind of lifestyle do you see yourself
settling into? How might the early phase
of your retirement look different from a
longer-term lifestyle?

MEANING, PURPOSE, AND A MEANINGFUL RETIREMENT

Having meaning and purpose in retirement is a general concern for many people as they leave their working lives behind. For some, a search for meaning and purpose even becomes the focus of the first part of retirement. The following sections of this book all have this aim in mind, to help you design a meaningful and fulfilling retirement. But what does this mean, to have meaning and purpose?

Meaning, purpose, and a meaningful life are things that we often talk about, and strive for; understandably, as they are a critical part of happiness and well-being.[1] We seem to know when they are missing in our lives, but may not know where to find them. Even researchers have a difficult time defining what we mean by these concepts.[2] With all of their complexity and ambiguity, it's no wonder they can feel so illusive when they are missing in our lives.

Meaningfulness is very much a personal experience. It is tied to our internal sense of self and our interpretation of events. It is about living authentically – expressing ourselves and living out personal attributes.[3] Researchers also describe it as a sense of coherence, significance, or fulfillment in our interpretation of events. Purpose is also very personal, but distinct in that it generally refers to goals, aims, or a sense of direction. Purpose therefore tends to be more future-oriented, while meaningfulness is more about the sense we make of past and present experiences.[4]

We could spend a great deal of time attempting to untangle these concepts. But for this purpose, we will stick to a few key considerations with regard to cultivating meaning and purpose in retirement, and then explore a few common sources of meaning and purpose.

1. **Meaning and purpose in day-to-day life contributes to a broader sense of meaning and purpose.**

Meaning and purpose may be thought of in terms of their scope, being either global (meaning/purpose *in life*) or specific (meaning/purpose *in day-to-day experiences*). Meaning and purpose in day-to-day activities contributes to a broader experience of meaning and purpose in life.[5] In other words, rather than beginning a search for meaning in life, one may find that focusing on meaningful activities contributes to a broader sense of meaning in life. Such activities tend to be experienced as positive, inspiring, and aligning with one's sense of self (see more in the chapter, *What You Do*).

Retirees also often talk about having a sense of purpose *for the day*. Interestingly, this appears to be associated with how we organize our time (as described in the section, *How You Structure It*). Retirees often describe the realization that they needed to create some structure for the day – a reason to get the day started. Without such structure, they lack motivation and a sense of purpose for the day; they quickly find days passing by without accomplishing things they intended to do. The simple act of committing to some activities or setting specific goals for the day may therefore serve to create that sense of purpose for the day, and perhaps a more general sense of purpose in life.

2. Meaning in life is about making sense of past, present, and future experiences.

One of the major elements of meaning in life is the sense you make of your experiences.[6] In the retirement transition, this also means making sense of your retirement, in the context of your life story. Whether or not your retirement involves challenges or major adjustments, it will involve change on some level. This change is experienced, perceived, and woven into the context of your other life experiences. It becomes part of your life story; and this life story forms a sense of meaning in life.

Of course, retirement may be experienced as more of a disruption than a predictable, or welcome, life transition. In these cases, it may be more difficult to make sense of this change as part of your life story. This is the challenge with any unanticipated disruption in life: they require us to make sense of events that were unanticipated, even unwanted, and rewrite old scripts.

One purpose of this book is to help you design a retirement lifestyle that aligns with who you are, and that fits in with your life story, even if that story is different from what you anticipated. In the first sections of this book, *The Beginning: Your Career* and *Your Retirement Vision*, you began crafting this story.

Your career forms the foundation for this next journey in retirement. Subsequent sections then serve to address more specific aspects of the transition that may help your personal vision materialize. What this involves, exactly, depends on your personal circumstances, hopes, and interests. For some, the sense of meaning in retirement may not require active reflection. Others, however, may benefit from taking time to reflect on how retirement aligns with, or refines their personal life story – from past to present, and future. Does retirement naturally follow from the story of your career (or other life experiences)? Perhaps, as you progress through this book, you will find that you are refining your career and retirement, to make sense of this transition.

3. **Goals and a sense of direction contribute to meaning and purpose.**

As mentioned earlier, purpose is often considered a component of meaning in life.[6] Purpose refers to a sense of direction and having highly valued goals. However, this may look different for retirees than it does for those in the midst of their careers. While some retirees continue to actively pursue new goals in retirement, others shift their focus from ideas of achievement or accomplishment, and instead focus more on experiences in the present moment – e.g., relaxation, family and relationships, and hobbies.

Nonetheless, a general sense of direction - perhaps a clear vision for this chapter in your life - may contribute to a sense of purpose and meaning in retirement. Again, progressing through this book may help you develop a general sense of direction for retirement. It is not necessarily about having a detailed plan; rather, a general vision and sense of what it may entail. To what extent are you interested in pursuing future-oriented goals in retirement versus focusing on the present? What might this entail?

4. Sources of meaning and purpose may shift and change over time.

Meaning and purpose are often described as overarching themes that create a central focus throughout our lives. Some people will experience this consistent theme throughout life. However, as we develop on different trajectories throughout our lives, others may find that their sense of meaning and purpose in life will evolve over time.[7] Frederic Hudson, for instance, describes the importance of "employing the appropriate core values at different times in the adult journey" (*p. 129, The Adult Years: Mastering the Art of Self-Renewal*).[8] For many people, retirement is a transition that involves a shift in core values. It may involve placing more value on family, health, or living life at a slower pace, and less value on things like productivity and achievement. Our values, interests, and other characteristics shift and change through different stages of life - what was important to you in adolescence may very well be quite different from what was most important to you in your 30's, and from what is most important to you now. These unique sets of values, interests, and other personal characteristics contribute to our experience of meaning and purpose.

What common factors contribute to meaning and purpose in life?

We discussed the role that day-to-day experiences play in our broader sense of meaning and purpose in life. We also discussed the personal nature of these experiences, as they are based in our personal characteristics, internal sense of self, and our interpretations of events. Finally, we discussed how sources of meaning and purpose may change over time. However, researchers have also explored specific factors, or types of involvements, that tend to be associated with a sense of meaning and purpose. These factors include generativity, family and other close relationships (a sense of belonging), religion and spirituality, personal growth and learning, achievement and accomplishment. Additionally, as is the concern of many retirees, work is often considered a source of meaning.

Work as a source of meaning and purpose. From Millennials to Baby Boomers, the trend today is to pursue meaningful work (and usually on more flexible terms). As we consider retirement, it's important to point out that it is not necessarily work itself that is meaningful, but specific characteristics of work that make it meaningful. Furthermore, as you'll see, many of these characteristics may be found in environments and activities outside of work as well. Some characteristics that contribute to meaningful work include:[9]

- Alignment with the self; reflecting personal motivations, values & beliefs[10]
- Sense of belonging and connectedness (with colleagues, leaders, or organization)
- Task identity – the ability to see the whole job/task through, from start to finish[11]
- Positive leadership – having leaders that develop and inspire others with a collective purpose, mission, or vision[9]
- Skill variety[11]
- Positive impact on others[9,11]

Generativity refers to involvement in activities that benefit future generations. One study found this to be an important coping mechanism for unemployed older adults.[12] In his book, *A New Purpose*, Ken Dychtwald also promotes the idea of going from "success to significance;" he describes significance in terms of giving back to younger generations or others in need.[13] Researchers also find that meaning in life is enhanced through activities that involve going beyond personal interests, to benefit others.[14] With a good deal of both work and life experience, retirees are in a position to provide some mentoring and guidance for younger generations.

Family and close relationships may be a significant source of meaning in life.[15] Close connections with others often provide meaning in the form of love and intimacy, sharing experiences, and providing and receiving positive feedback and support. Making it through difficult times with others may also contribute to feelings of meaningfulness. One study found that family and close relationships were a primary source of meaning for many older adults, more so than for younger adults.[16] For them, meaning in life was more about the quality of connections with others than the quantity.

Religion and spirituality offer frameworks for understanding life, and may be a primary source of meaning and purpose.[17] This may range from active participation with a religious affiliation to more general spiritual practices such as meditation or yoga.

Personal growth and learning may also be significant sources of meaning in life.[18] This refers to things like developing your strengths and overcoming weaknesses, tackling goals and challenges, or lifelong learning. While this tends to be a focus for younger groups,[15] many people also see retirement as an opportunity to develop themselves in new ways.

Achievement and accomplishment is similar to personal growth and learning, but speaks specifically to accomplishments and meeting goals. We tend to associate achievement with career and work, but whether or not we are working, the pursuit of challenges may be meaningful and important (see the next chapter, *What You Do*). Additionally, previous attainment of goals may be an ongoing source of meaning in life.

* * *

For the meaning of life differs from man to man, from day to day and from hour to hour. What matters, therefore, is not the meaning of life in general but rather the specific meaning of a person's life at a given moment.

—Viktor Frankl (1959, p. 49)[19]

REFLECTIVE QUESTIONS

Reflecting over the course of your life, are there any underlying themes that have remained an important part of you and your life? What, if any, shifts and changes do you recall in your priorities, interests, or general focus in life?

What do you feel contributes, or will contribute to a meaningful retirement?

WHO YOU ARE

"People are what they do, and what people do effects every aspect of who they are. For good or ill, we are known and we know ourselves by the work we do"
—Al Gini (1998, p. 708)[1]

With the amount of time we devote to our work role, it is bound to become an important part of who we are, and how we see ourselves. For some, work may be more of a means to an end. Others, however, find their work to be an integral part of their identity. Leaving behind such a fundamental part of you can be extremely daunting; for some, it even leads to feelings of bereavement and emptiness. Many retirees, however, utilize strategies to support identity-related adjustments in retirement. Whether you experience minor feelings of loss, or more significant distress, you may find that one or more of these strategies will help you navigate a smooth transition.

Shifting your priorities and focus

Jim worked for the same company for 29 years, fighting for it when things were tough, and feeling a sense of pride when he helped turn things around. He was not just devoted to work; he was committed to the company's success. So while he saved for retirement, he wasn't really sure if he would ever actually retire—he enjoyed work that much.

Then, as Jim approached his 62nd birthday, he began to have a change of heart. Once again, things were in a state of flux at work, and he was starting to wonder if he should spend more time with his family. His children were finishing college and he looked back on all the events he missed because of work. His wife had always been understanding and supportive of his career, but she would have liked him around a bit more. Although he would not really be able to make up for lost time, he felt that, with comfortable retirement savings, it was time to start shifting gears.

Retirement was not an easy move. Jim's colleagues had been like a surrogate family, and retirement meant leaving this family behind to focus on his real family. He often considered returning to work, with a less demanding schedule. But he gave it some time, made some adjustments to his daily routine, and soon found a satisfying balance between family time and other engaging involvements, such as volunteering at a local nature preserve.

Many people find that their personal values, priorities, and motivation naturally evolve as they approach retirement. Factors such as personal health, family, or new life experiences often become a greater priority. Many people also place less emphasis on things like productivity, achievement, or power as they approach this stage. Generally speaking, people begin placing greater value on quality of life as they near retirement.

Whether or not you have experienced a similar change in priorities in your own transition, you might want to consider retirement as an opportunity to shift your focus to other priorities and life experiences. Consider the things that retirement will allow you to focus on—what interests and priorities have you not had enough time for?

It is also important to note that even after retirement, our interests and priorities continue to evolve, so it's worth revisiting this from time to time. Once completed, the table below can offer a useful reference point - a means to track any shift in priorities and the changes you have made to accommodate this.

REFLECTIVE QUESTIONS

Personal Values and Priorities

List five things you see as most important in your work, life outside of work, and retirement.

Work	Life outside of work	Retirement

What potential retirement activities will align with your priorities in life outside of work and in retirement?

What other aspects of life will retirement allow you to focus on or spend more time on?

Maintaining important work-related aspects of who you are

Sue enjoyed a career in nursing; what she found most rewarding was helping others improve their lives in some way. Nonetheless, when she retired she had little interest in any part-time work or formal volunteer work. Instead, she decided to volunteer her time, on an informal basis, to those in need of care or attention. She helped neighbors get to doctor's appointments, picked-up prescriptions when they were unwell, or went for coffee with someone that needed companionship. This was not how she spent all of her time; she also made a point of maintaining time for her other interests. But this was a way for her to continue one of the things she found most rewarding about work: making a difference in other people's lives.

Continuing to use work-related skills, knowledge, and experience is important for many retirees.[2] In some cases this means continuing work on more flexible terms, or pursuing new forms of work. Others have found activities outside of work that utilize their skills and expertise in new ways.

The aspect of work that Sue, in the story above, was most interested in was continuing to help others. Sometimes this involved her skills and knowledge in nursing, such as when she attended doctor's visits with elderly friends. But in reality, the part of nursing that she connected with most, whether or not it involved using medical knowledge, was her compassion and people skills.

As you consider ways to maintain important work-related skills, you might start by identifying those aspects of work that you connected most with. Then, allow some space to think creatively, and consider ways that you might continue to engage these skills in retirement.

REFLECTIVE QUESTIONS

Which aspects of work do you personally connect with? Which are you interested in continuing?

What skills, knowledge, and experience do you bring to work? Which of these do you find rewarding to implement at work?

Which work-related values and priorities would continue to be important to you in retirement (refer back to your reflections in the previous section, *Shifting your priorities and focus*)?

Diversifying your portfolio for life

The increasing stress and demands of teaching wore on Helen, causing her to fall ill and be out of work for several weeks. As she recovered, she realized she needed to stop work and start taking care of herself, to avoid irreversible damage to her health and wellbeing. It was sooner than expected, but it was time for her to start a new chapter.

With the time Helen devoted to work, caring for her health had been put on the back burner. Her daughter's wedding was approaching and, being a little overweight, she thought retirement would be an opportunity to focus on her health and fitness. Fortunately, an acquaintance of hers had always been very fit and was excited to help someone else benefit from what she learned over the years.

Ten months into retirement, Helen had discovered an entirely new way of living, and a new side of herself. She achieved her goal weight, by completely changing her eating habits and exercising regularly, for the first time in her life. More importantly, she had more energy and felt substantially better.

Retirement opens the door to opportunities for personal growth, and pursuing new hobbies, interests, and life experiences. If you have had little time outside of work to devote to your own needs, retirement may give you the opportunity to do so. For some people, this could mean gaining new life experiences through travel. Others may learn a new skill or pursue a new hobby. For Helen, retirement was an opportunity to make a personal transformation by focusing on her health and fitness.

Despite seeing retirement as a time of new possibilities, many retirees tend to continue with the same leisure interests they had before retirement. Perhaps the motivation to instigate such new pursuits is initially lacking, or perceived to be too much effort. It would therefore be advisable to take some small steps to 'get the ball rolling' and then set specific goals within a time frame, to keep check on your progress. This is likely to be a more effective approach than waiting for the motivation to arrive, or for new opportunities to present themselves. If possible, make the necessary inquiries before you retire, or as early as possible in retirement – you can begin to connect and engage with new activities before you disconnect from work.

WHAT DO YOU DO?

The way in which work becomes a part of how we see ourselves, and how others see us is perhaps most readily apparent through introductions. Something many people do not think about as they approach retirement is how they will answer the question commonly asked when you meet someone: *What do you do?*

Some retirees have no qualms with simply answering, "I'm retired." For others, however, this may set in motion a whole wave of emotions, realizations, and questions. *If you have been an engineer for thirty years and then retire, are you still an engineer? You certainly still feel like an engineer...*

The work that you dedicated such a great deal of your life to has probably become an important part of who you are - this usually does not change with retirement. Our past experiences and personal stories continue to shape who we are today. Because of this, you may be happy to tell people what you have done for work, *"I am a retired nurse."* Or, you might also add to this by saying a bit about what you are doing now, or how you spend your time in retirement. Are you pursuing a new career or even going back to study? Are you taking this time to focus on family, spending time with your spouse or grandchildren? Or are you simply taking this time to explore your personal interests without the constraints and stresses of work?

Another question you might ask yourself is—if you had a business card in retirement, what would it say? In fact, some retirees do create their own business cards as a way to exchange details with new contacts.

However you choose to respond, you might think about preparing yourself with an answer that resonates with you at the time. What answer would help others get to know you?

WHAT YOU DO

How will I be engaged in something that gives meaning and purpose to everyday life? It's not just about earning money for me. I want to do something worthwhile and useful.

Professor, nearing retirement

Free time, itself, does not necessarily lead to a satisfying retirement. *It's how you use your time that matters.* The usual advice is to stay busy, develop hobbies, get involved in volunteer work, and keep your brain active. For the most part, these things have been linked to greater adjustment and wellbeing in retirement.[1] But what about the quality of your personal experience with these activities?

Most people are looking to not only stay active in retirement, but to stay involved in activities that they find positive, meaningful, and challenging. Such activities are generally referred to as *engaging activities*; and they also contribute to retirement adjustment and satisfaction, even more so than by simply staying active.[2] It may be the case that work lacked a sense of true meaning – that it was a means to make money and pay the bills. If so, retirement could present the opportunity to invest time in more worthwhile pursuits and instate a greater sense of worth.

The importance of engagement, and not just involvement, in activities was clearly demonstrated in one study by the Sloan Center on Aging & Work at Boston College.[3] Researchers examined participation in paid work, volunteer work, caregiving, and education, and found that being *engaged* in these activities was linked to greater wellbeing, when compared with simple involvement in them. In other words, those who were involved simply for the sake of filling their time had lower wellbeing compared to those that found these activities to be positive, meaningful, or inspiring.

Furthermore, those who were involved in paid work, volunteer work, caregiving, or education simply for the sake of filling time also experienced lower wellbeing compared to those who chose not to participate in these activities at all. Keeping busy and filling your time in retirement may therefore be less important than identifying a few activities that you find meaningful, positive, and inspiring.

Rather than simply filling your days, focus on a few highly engaging and rewarding activities.

Based on research and conversations with retirees, three types of engaging activities appear to be an important part of retirement adjustment and satisfaction: meaningful activities, challenging activities (those that create flow), and activities involving impact and contribution. As you consider your choice of activities you may be able to identify ones that fall into several of these categories. For instance, volunteering may be meaningful while also involving impact and contribution.

MEANINGFUL ACTIVITIES

Janet was involved in many different activities in retirement, some with her husband and some without. One of her new projects was particularly meaningful for her at this point in her life: she was beginning to write memoirs of her mother's experiences during World War II. She heard stories throughout her life, and she felt they should be recorded and shared as an important piece of history. This was also an opportunity for her to explore more of her own family history.

Most people are interested in not only staying active in retirement, but doing something meaningful – whether it is through some form of paid work or other involvements. Meaningful activities are an important part of the retirement transition, just as they are in other phases of life.[4] Such activities bring about benefits to health, happiness, and the ability to cope with adversities.[5] They also contribute to a more general sense of meaning in life (as we explored in the chapter, *Meaning, Purpose, and a Meaningful Retirement*). So what exactly are meaningful activities?

We seem to know when something is experienced as meaningful, and when it is not. When we are lacking meaning in our day-to-day activities, the idea of finding something meaningful may feel a bit illusive, intangible, and difficult to grasp. This may be, at least in part, because it is linked to our internal sense of self rather than some externally defined activity (e.g., volunteer work). In other words, your individual characteristics play a role in whether or not particular involvements are experienced as meaningful. Activities that align with your personal life history, as well as your values, interests, and goals are more likely to be experienced as meaningful, important, and worthwhile.[6] Therefore, pursuits that are experienced as meaningful by you will probably be quite different from what others experience as meaningful. With this in mind, the search for meaningful activities may start by reflecting within, rather than sifting through 'what's out there.'

Use your experience of what you have found meaningful in the past, to identify ways to implement this in retirement. Also consider your current values, priorities, and personal interests.

REFLECTIVE QUESTIONS

You began this reflective process in the last chapter, *Who You Are*, by reflecting on your current values and priorities. The reflective questions in this section expand on this by exploring potential activities that align with important aspects of who you are.

What are your top personal interests?
List the things you find intriguing, inspiring, or enjoyable. These may be work or non-work related. Then rate your level of interest on a scale of 1 to 10 (1 = not very interested; 10 = very interested).

Interests	Rated Interest (1 to 10)
1.	
2.	
3.	
4.	
5.	
6.	

Which of these would you like to explore in retirement?

Now, referencing your interests above and your personal priorities from the previous section on *Who You Are*, what potential retirement activities align with your top personal interests and priorities?

Priorities and Interests	Potential Retirement Activities
1.	
2.	
3.	
4.	
5.	
6.	

CHALLENGING ACTIVITIES AND FLOW

A common concern about retirement is missing the challenge that work provides. Most people want to stay active and engaged in retirement, both physically and mentally. This is a legitimate concern, as opportunities for problem-solving, learning, and other such activities are often found in the work environment. These activities are often a source of stress; yet, at the same time, they tend to contribute to feelings of mastery and personal control.[7] Replacing such experiences may therefore be an important element of adjusting to retirement.

Challenging activities push us outside of our comfort zone, stretching our existing skills and abilities in order to accomplish a goal. This can be a positive way to boost confidence in our ability, and gain a sense of satisfaction. Rather than being imposed from the outside, retirement calls us to be more proactive in pursuing activities that provide a challenge—whether physical, intellectual, or both. Examples of this might be learning a new language, participating in a team sport, running a half-marathon – whatever resonates as a worthy challenge for you.

Flow: Getting in the Zone

Jim sat down on his bench in the garden and quenched his thirst with lukewarm water that had been sitting in the sun. It was almost time for dinner and he was starting to realize just how hungry he was. Something about gardening really captures him now and then. He gets into the zone, sets out with a new project in mind, and it's as if nothing else exists. This also happened at work, when writing code, though that was a bit different. He always enjoyed being carried off, almost to another world, when he was deeply engaged with a project. This usually happened when he had a few hours set aside to really focus on a particular problem, yet to be solved. His work often commanded his full attention, as opposed to multi-tasking or jumping from one thing to the next. Now, he discovered that same feeling of being 'in the zone' through a few different activities—gardening was one, as was writing and going out on strenuous hikes.

A concept related to activities that provide a challenge is that of flow.[8] Flow is a psychological state that you may recognize as feeling 'in the zone,' as Jim experienced in the story above. It is a state of mind in which you become completely immersed and absorbed by what you are doing. You may tune out things going on around you, lose track of time, and even forget about other things going on in your life—worries, concerns, or responsibilities—at least while you are absorbed in the activity.

Flow tends to occur in an activity where there is an appropriate balance between the level of challenge involved and your skill level. In other words, it tends to occur in activities that are a bit challenging, but not impossible. It is also a spontaneous state that is often characterized by a deep sense of enjoyment. When people describe being at their happiest, they often describe the state of flow. Because of this, activities that tend to elicit flow may play a positive role in retirement adjustment and wellbeing.

Flow is most likely to occur with challenging activities; however, if you are developing an entirely new skill, you may find you have to climb the initial learning curve before you are really able to get into the zone. Either way, identifying activities that challenge your current abilities and push you just a bit outside of your comfort zone may contribute to a satisfying retirement. The key point is to raise the bar a bit higher with some of your involvements. There may be activities you already enjoy outside of work that you can develop further, or you might start a new pursuit that requires the development of entirely new skills.

REFLECTIVE QUESTIONS

What activities do you enjoy that involve the pursuit of success, accomplishment, or mastery?

If you are not currently involved in such activities, what are some potential retirement activities of this type?

What skills might you like to develop (or further develop) in retirement? How might you develop these skills?

Are there activities, outside of work, in which you have experienced flow?

Do you ever find yourself heavily immersed in certain activities, perhaps losing track of time or forgetting about other things going on around you?

IMPACT AND CONTRIBUTION

I've had a lot of benefits in my career, but now I have to give back in the coming years. I'd like to help at least a portion of those people who are really in need. So that's part of my retirement, giving back to the developing countries, giving back all my skills and experience.
–Semi-Retired Accountant

Broadly speaking, retirement is no longer seen as a time of leisure, disengagement, and withdrawal, but rather a time of active involvement.[9] Many retirees wish to contribute to something beyond their personal interests; to make a difference in some way. Activities that involve being productive, making a contribution, or adding value to others appear to be an important part of retirement for many people, supporting self-esteem and feelings of usefulness.[10]

Some contribute their time and energy through volunteer work and community involvement (which have been found to support retirement adjustment and satisfaction[11]). However, volunteer work is not for everyone - there may be other pursuits that still involve having an impact and making a contribution in some way. For instance, some people may focus on contributing to their family. Others may enjoy both the flexibility and reward of informal volunteering—

helping neighbors, friends, or acquaintances. Personal projects, such as art or writing a book, may also be a rewarding way to leave one's mark.

As you consider activities involving impact and contribution in your retirement, you may want to think about your values and interests, as well as the personal skills and strengths that you would like to put into action.

REFLECTIVE QUESTIONS

What kind of impact would you like to have in retirement? What kind of mark would you like to leave on the world or on others?

This may be on any level. For instance, would you like to have an impact on a more personal level with family, friends, or acquaintances (e.g., as a form of support)? Would you like to make a difference for younger generations? Or have an impact on a local organization, the local community, or a particular cause? Given your unique skills, experiences, and qualities, what might you do to make a difference in the world, or for others?

WHO IS INVOLVED

Frank felt his title, as coordinator, was an accurate depiction of his primary role at work - motivating others to work effectively with one another in order to accomplish a common goal. This was also the most rewarding aspect of work for him. He thrived on his ability to work with people from different backgrounds, with different perspectives, and encourage them to work collaboratively.

However, Frank had few social contacts outside of work. He maintained communication with former colleagues that were also retiring, but they had all scattered to different locations. In his time off, he usually had projects around the house and spent time with his wife. In fact, he was concerned about stepping on his wife's toes around the house once he retired.

Fast forward several years into retirement, and Frank was heavily involved with his family. He was particularly fond of his new role as a grandparent. This offered a replacement for the time previously spent focusing on work. He also maintained active involvement in professional organizations and occasionally volunteered for non-profit organizations. Through these pursuits, he was able to interact with likeminded people. He missed the professional interactions at work, but overall he was happy with his new social circle.

Positive and healthy relationships play a critical role in our health and wellbeing throughout our entire lifespan.[1] They enhance our feelings of self-worth, and have a positive impact on our physical health by reducing the effects of stress.[2] Because work is often a significant source of social groups and day-to-day interaction, our social involvements seem to be particularly important in retirement.[3]

Missing co-workers and colleagues is one of the most common complaints about retirement.[4] More specifically, however, retirees find they miss the unique types of interactions they had in the work-place, such as collaborating and problem-solving.[5] They often report their surprise in finding that such interactions are difficult to recreate in retirement.

One recent study of older workers and retirees in England found that, for retirees in particular, social group memberships impact not only quality of life, but also physical health and even longevity.[6] Those who belonged to fewer groups after retirement (than while they were working) had an increased risk of poor-health compared to those that maintained an equal number of social groups. Furthermore, the effects of social group memberships on health and longevity were comparable to that of physical exercise. This suggests we should consider our social involvements as part of a health regimen.

Does this mean retirement is bad for health? Not exactly. As we've been exploring throughout this book, retirement clearly involves some life changes and personal adjustments. While some of those changes may have health benefits (e.g., reduced stress, time for exercise), findings from the abovementioned research simply highlight the importance of the social side of retirement.[7] Joining new groups and maintaining membership in existing social groups, outside of work, will likely support quality of life and health in this transition.

In addition to wider social groups, your close support network and family relationships may play a crucial role in the retirement transition. In particular, spousal relationships often go through unique adjustments when one or both partners retire. Strategies for managing these adjustments are explored later in this chapter. But first, we'll look at three important considerations for the social side of your retirement: understanding your preferences for social interaction, making a conscious effort to stay socially active, and identifying your support network.

Understanding your preferences for social interaction.

As individuals, we have very different preferences for different *types* of interaction, as well as *amounts* of social interaction. The most common distinction is between introversion and extraversion.[8] Introverts tend to thrive in solitude and enjoy a few close relationships. Extraverts, on the other hand, thrive in social settings and enjoy having contact with many different people. Understanding where you lie on the spectrum from introversion to extraversion may help you gauge the extent to which social interaction will be an important part of your retirement. It's important to remember, however, that even introverts are social beings, and some social interaction is beneficial to wellbeing.

Additionally, you might consider the specific types of interactions you tend to find most enjoyable or rewarding. For instance, do you enjoy serious intellectual conversations, collaborating with others on projects, or more light-hearted socializing at the local coffee shop? Dr. Niklas Steffens and his colleagues emphasize the role that social groups play in our sense of identity.[6] It may not only be important to join new groups, but to join groups that you identify with, or that are meaningful to you. Your involvement with these groups will also support identity adjustments in retirement.

REFLECTIVE QUESTIONS

How much social interaction is right for you? Do you prefer interacting with many different people or really getting to know a few people?

Personality inventories measuring introversion and extraversion might shed some light on your personal tendencies in these areas. Myers-Briggs Type Indicator (MBTI) is one instrument that measures introversion and extraversion, along with other personality traits. You can complete the MBTI online and receive feedback at www.mbtionline.com

Most of us fall in between the extremes, so it will likely require a bit of trial and error to find the right fit for you in retirement. As you explore this, note whether solitude or social interactions leave you feeling tired, or energized and inspired. The ideal is to find a balance that's right for you.

What types of interactions do you enjoy? On a scale of 1 to 10, rate the extent to which you enjoy the following types of interactions (1 = Least Enjoyable; 10 = Most Enjoyable).

Interactions that Involve . . .	Rated Enjoyment
Mingling informally	
Competition and challenge	
Physical activities or sports (e.g., golf, tennis, cycling)	
Other games (e.g., poker, chess)	
Humor and joking	
Working on projects with others	
Collaborating with others on a common goal	
Sharing and discussing common interests	
Meeting for a meal or drink	

Interactions that Involve . . .	Rated Enjoyment
Entertaining others	
Performing with or for others (e.g., music, theater)	
Debate on controversial topics	
Intellectual conversations	
Conversations on personal topics	
Helping others	
Learning from or with others	
Other types of interactions not listed:	

What types of social interactions did you rate as most enjoyable? And what potential retirement activities would involve these types of interactions?

Make a conscious effort in your social life.

Work typically creates a structured environment, requiring interactions with others. Close bonds also develop between co-workers as a result of tackling challenges together. Without this structured work environment, however, retirees sometimes find they have to rely on their own initiative to start interactions and develop relationships. It may come as a surprise that it takes more time and effort to develop and maintain relationships. For some, this is easier and more natural than for others.

Those that join social groups outside of work, before actually retiring, find that these connections help to bridge the gap between work and retirement. Although they are often informal, these relationships may be a valuable source of support during the transitional phase. Of course, joining new social groups while working full time is not always easy, but where possible, it is likely to help with your adjustment to retirement. Once in retirement, it is also advisable to make a conscious effort to involve yourself in social activities. For instance, you might make commitments to participate in regular social or community-based activities.

REFLECTIVE QUESTIONS

What social activities and relationships are you currently involved in outside of work?

How might you maintain contact with your professional community or associates?

If you belong to any professional organizations outside of work, you might want to consider maintaining your involvement in these groups after retirement. What other social groups might you join in retirement?

Identify your support network.

Support networks are those relationships that we may not really think about and may even take for granted; but they become critical when we face challenging times. Even those who report little difficulty with retirement also describe their supportive relationships as a critical part of their adjustment.[9] Friends and family tend to be a strong source of support. Additionally, social groups you join while working and then continue after retirement may offer an important sense of belonging and continuity. It's important to note that the support needed may range from simple companionship to direct emotional assistance – so it's worth considering who you might turn to in each case.

Retirement Tip: If you are planning to move in retirement, also consider how you will maintain contact with an existing support network, as well as how you will develop new supportive connections.

REFLECTIVE QUESTIONS

Who will you turn to for support in your transition to retirement, if need be? If you have difficulty coming up with people, consider groups or professionals such as counselors.

Keep in mind that you may find supportive interactions and connections in more informal places. Many people find social groups will offer enough support in retirement. (If you don't feel comfortable discussing such matters with your personal network, there are professionals, such as counselors, who offer support and the opportunity to talk through any difficulties.)

FAMILY AND SPOUSAL ADJUSTMENTS

Amanda knew her husband was due to retire and was looking forward to them spending more time together. Her husband, Gary, held a very senior position in a rail company and worked extremely long hours on very high-profile projects. Due to the nature of his work, and the confidential information Gary was privy to, the company had a policy of all or nothing retirement. Reducing hours / days slowly wasn't an option as it ran the risk of an employee being approached to work for a rival company, while still having access to their existing company's documentation.

Gary therefore had the date set to retire, but as the day drew closer, Amanda noticed that he made little comment about it – or what he planned to do after he retired. He was in denial.

On the day Gary retired, he came home with his personal items from work and left them in a box in the spare room. And then he started...doing nothing. He sat around the house, clearly in a state of shock that his career had come to an end. Amanda tried to talk to him, to suggest activities they could take part in together, or things Gary could do independently. He agreed, in principle, but when the time came, he made excuses and stayed at home.

Amanda was beside herself – having led an active life in and outside of their home, she now had her husband moping about all day every day, clearly showing signs of depression and bringing her down too. Their relationship suffered – she looks back at that being a very dark time and is surprised and relieved that their marriage survived.

After the first year, things began to slowly improve. Gary started exercising regularly and then took a part-time position at the local Citizens Advice Bureau, using his considerable knowledge to help others.

Retirement is more than just an individual transition – it's a family transition.[10] It is an opportunity to focus more on family, if that is what you want; but it may also require a bit of adjustment for everyone involved. Your family will have an impact on your retirement experience, and vice versa - your retirement will also have an impact on your family. Adjustment problems faced by one partner also tend to affect the quality of the other partner's retirement experience,[11] as Gary and Amanda experienced, in the story above. It may also signal changes in your relationship, and the roles each of you fulfills. Just having you home, for instance, may be a significant change in routine for other family members. Addressing changes as early as possible will certainly help, as will ongoing communication as you settle into retirement.

For those without family close-by, and who are either single, separated, or widowed, retirement may offer the opportunity to reconnect socially and perhaps even meet a companion to share your time with. The following sections focus largely on how to approach retirement within a family context, but may also contain useful points on communication in general – with existing or future personal relationships.

Grandparenting

Grandparenting is an important, and very rewarding role for many retirees. In addition to the close emotional connection, it can provide a natural and positive identity transition, from being a 'worker' to becoming a 'grandparent.' Grandparent relation-ships also offer a number of benefits on both sides, including intergenerational connections and exposure, reduced depressive symptoms for the retiree, and pro-social behavior among children.[12] Of course, such intergenerational relationships may also be developed outside of grandparent relationships. For instance, one retiree focused her time on writing children's books and conducting workshops in schools, despite never having children of her own.

You will, however, want to consider the extent to which you will invest your time and energy to caring for your grandchildren in retirement. As you explore the areas outlined in this book, you may develop a sense of how to balance these other important aspects of your retirement with your role as a grandparent.

Clarifying Plans, Expectations, and Boundaries

Family members will develop their own ideas and expectations for your retirement, and how you will spend your newfound freedom. Misunderstandings between retirees and their loved ones are often about the retirees' availability, and willingness, to provide support in terms of time or money. Your children calling on you for financial support may not fit into the budget you have outlined for retirement. Further to this, spending your free time doing favors for others may not be how you envisioned life in retirement. Not all grandparents are interested in looking after their grandchildren on a regular basis. You may, therefore, be able avoid misunderstanding, and potential ill-feeling, by openly communicating your own plans and expectations.

A surprising number of couples also fail to communicate their retirement hopes, plans, and expectations with one another. According to a 2015 Couples Retirement Study by Fidelity Investments,

72% of couples say they communicate very well; however, there seemed to be a disconnect between couples in terms of their retirement age, retirement savings, and retirement lifestyle.[13] You can imagine the kind of problems such misunderstandings can create. Many people, it seems, simply assume that their partner feels the same way as they do, sharing the same vision for retirement. However, rather than making this assumption, communicating with your partner about your visions for retirement helps prevent frustration and disappointment on both sides.

Timing Retirement with Your Partner

Your partner's employment status at the time of your retirement will have an impact on how your relationship evolves and the choices you both make. If you happen to retire at the same time as your partner, you may have big ideas for how you plan to spend retirement together: perhaps moving to a new area, traveling, or simply enjoying more time as a couple. Whatever the plan is, you will be diving headfirst into retirement at the same time - dealing not only with your personal adjustment to retirement, but also with big changes in your relationship. This may also mean, however, that you are both available to support one another through the transition. Although it is a big change, many couples find it to be a positive one, particularly when both partners maintain open communication.

Retiring at different times (or retiring when your partner has been managing things at home) may lead to a unique set of experiences. If you are retiring first, then ideally you will begin to develop your own interests, as well as possible shared ones, before your partner retires. Without your own interests and involvements, you may be more prone to boredom and loneliness while your partner is still busy at work. Again, this is usually difficult for both partners. When your partner retires, they may be surprised if you already have an active and busy life that does not include them. They may also need to develop their own interests and activities, as well as join you with shared activities. It may be important for them to understand that you have, and will, carry on with some of your own involvements in retirement.

Managing Changes with Your Partner: Time, Shared Space, and Household Responsibilities
As is true of most retired couples, you will probably spend more time with your partner than ever before. This can be both a good and a bad thing, depending on the quality of your relationship and how you manage the changes. Retired couples often emphasize the importance of balancing time together with time

spent on independent interests and activities.[14] Even if spending more time with your partner is a priority in your retirement, maintaining some of your own activities, and identity, may benefit your relationship. Some couples are pleased to find that this also fosters new topics of conversation when they are together. Although we do not like to think about it, having independent interests and involvements may also be an important part of coping when faced with the loss of a partner - allowing the surviving partner to experience some form of continuity.

Increased time together also means more time where you are both at home. Couples often describe feeling 'on top of one another' after they retire. And women (or men) that have stayed home often find that their space feels invaded when their partner retires. Both you and your partner may find that you would like some time alone in the house, to do your own thing. Some couples arrange for each partner to leave the house at certain times, or certain days, perhaps to pursue those independent interests. That way, you are both able to enjoy some quiet time at home.

Finally, as you are both around the house more often, you may find you need to renegotiate household responsibilities. Many retired couples report a shift in household roles after retiring. Some prefer to do certain tasks and may actually feel that their role is being encroached upon when their partner begins helping out. Alternatively, some people find they want the help but that they also need to adjust their expectations about how things are done. Such changes can actually be one of the more difficult aspects of retirement. Of course, with open communication, it should be possible to negotiate a solution that works for you both, and allows you to settle into a new pattern and lifestyle.

Keep Communication Going

Communication is a critical part of a relationship at any point. It may be particularly important in retirement, however, as you are spending more time together; and there is more time to focus on issues (with retirement or in the relationship). A minor nuisance - such as one partner watching the morning news when the other would prefer some peace and quiet - can quickly chip away at marital satisfaction, creating a domino effect where other issues arise. Rather than waiting until minor issues turn into more significant problems, maintaining an open dialog may foster a more supportive and nurturing relationship. Ideally, both partners will openly express thoughts, experiences, and expectations on retirement and possible changes in the relationship.

It's important to remember that, generally, people do settle well into a new routine; changes that feel initially unsettling, probably just need a little getting used to. Encouraging your partner to speak openly about any concerns, and doing so yourself, will offer the opportunity to discuss ideas for making positive changes. It also makes room to ask for, and offer, support and reassurance – which is crucial during any phase of adjustment.

REFLECTIVE QUESTIONS

How might you and your spouse maintain an open dialog about your experiences and emotions around retirement?

The following questions may be points to discuss with your partner as you consider retirement:

- What is your vision for your retirement?
- Will you retire together or at different times?
- If one partner wants or needs to continue work, what new involvements will the retired partner pursue with their additional free time?
- How will you spend time together?
- What pursuits will you enjoy independently?

- What are your expectations in terms of household responsibilities?
- What are your expectations in terms of shared versus personal space around the house?

HOW YOU STRUCTURE IT

Iris closed her laptop and walked to the kitchen to make a cup of coffee. She already had coffee earlier in the morning but was starting to drag her feet again. Glancing at the clock, she realized it was 2pm—just like that, the day was passing by, and she hadn't yet left the house.

When she was still working, Iris very much looked forward to taking it easy in retirement. She anxiously awaited the freedom to sleep in as late as she wanted and to have the day to spend as she pleased. However, three months into retirement, she was starting to get fed-up with her life of leisure. She was typically a very active and energetic person, but many days found herself sitting around doing nothing. Not feeling like her usual self, she realized she needed to get involved in something again, something that would structure her days, get her moving in the mornings, and provide a sense of purpose for the day.

She began to keep an eye out for things she could get involved in and soon found a local book club. This would at least get her out and about once in a while. One thing led to another and she was soon volunteering one day a week with the animal shelter and meeting with a group that got together for walks in the area. More and more opportunities came up, from which she would pick and choose what she was interested in. Most importantly, she found a balance between the freedom she longed for in retirement and the focus she found she also needed for the days. Even on days when she didn't have any commitments, she now found herself much more active, pursuing other interests. She was back to her normal, enthusiastic self and doing things she really loved, surrounded by nature and other likeminded people.

An abundance of free time is one of the most highly anticipated benefits of retirement. We anxiously await the freedom from overly rigid and demanding schedules, and the ability to do what we want, when we want. Ironically, however, an abundance of unstructured free time can also be problematic.[1] Some people struggle with a lack of motivation or sense of purpose for the day. Without structure or external obligations, some retirees also report feeling that there is a void in their lives. Others struggle with the opposite problem, feeling bombarded and overwhelmed with demands on their time. These retirees find that some time management is actually needed in order to manage the requests coming in from others, and to maintain time for themselves.

So, it appears that a balance between an overly structured routine and an abundance of unstructured free time is optimal. In fact, free time management has been linked to greater quality of life in retirement.[2] In support of this finding, retirees often report that re-establishing some kind of routine was an important part of their adjustment to life in retirement.[3]

But what exactly do we mean by free time management?

It's about flexibility and spontaneity versus structure and routine, and finding the right balance between the two. What this actually looks like in retirement will vary from person to person based on individual preferences for routine, plans, and structure. It may range from a few regular commitments, to having clear plans for the day ahead. Below are some general strategies to consider implementing, in order to balance free time and a degree of structure. These strategies are then followed by further contemplation of issues with both boredom and an overly busy retirement.

1. Commit to some regular activities (e.g., weekly involvements).

Having some routine and structure with your time does not necessarily mean scheduling every hour of every day. A simple way to create a bit of structure is to commit to some regular activities - social activities, perhaps? This may be a few days a week, or even a few days a month. Commitment to regular activities will help to create some focus to your days and/or weeks in retirement.

2. Develop a new routine involving things you enjoy on a daily basis.

Routines do not have to be boring. Perhaps there are things you would like to be doing on a daily basis or at least with some regularity? For instance, you may enjoy starting the morning with a newspaper and coffee, a bike ride, or gardening. Whatever it is, some kind of routine will help to get the day started.

3. Set goals or priorities for your free time.

Personal goals and priorities also help to create some focus and motivate us to take action in our free time. For example, you might have a goal to spring clean one week, walk two miles each day, or finish a book by the end of the month. If you have general aims, such as a healthier lifestyle, consider more specific, actionable goals within a specific timeframe. If there's a goal you really have your mind set on, you might also want to consider making your goals SMARTER: specific (simple), measurable, achievable, relevant, time-bound, evaluated, and rewarded.[4]

4. Set boundaries.

In finding the right balance between a busy lifestyle and one with an overabundance of unscheduled free time, you may also need to set some boundaries with others in terms of how you spend your time. This might mean letting others know what you are or are not willing to do; or simply knowing when to say no. You might wish to reserve evenings for dinner with the family, or mornings for exercise or other routines.

Or, you might need to set boundaries in terms of the things you get involved in, such as volunteer opportunities or helping out family members. Prepare a response to requests you are unsure about, and if you are already involved in something you'd rather not be, do not be afraid to back out and protect your own time.

REFLECTIVE QUESTIONS

Referencing your personal priorities and interests, in the chapter *Who You Are*, consider the type of goals that you might set with your free time. What priorities will create some focus for your time in retirement?

What regular activities will you be involved in (e.g., daily, weekly, monthly)?

What will be part of your daily routine? Will you have a routine for the week that is different from the weekend?

For instance, will you wake up earlier during the week, have an exercise routine, be involved in groups or volunteer work?

THE MEANING OF LEISURE TIME

Another experience people often find surprising in their retirement is changes in the meaning of their leisure activities and free time. Weekends and hobbies often no longer have the same meaning as they did in the context of, and in contrast to, a busy working life. For instance, one retiree described how visiting his summer cottage no longer offered the same pleasure after retirement. Researchers in one study also found that administrative activities, such as paying bills, were less burdensome for retirees than for workers - as you might guess, because they have more free time![5]

ISSUES WITH BOREDOM

Boredom is a common concern for those approaching retirement. People will often ask those nearing retirement, *what will you do with all that free time - will you get bored?* The boredom people fear often does not actually materialize. In fact, many find the opposite to be true as they become quite busy in retirement. Nonetheless, boredom remains a concern, and an issue for some retirees.

What leads to boredom in retirement, and how might it be avoided?

Boredom is typically associated with not having enough things to do to fill one's time. Although we try to avoid it, it may not always be a bad thing. Some researchers have found that boring tasks actually increase subsequent curiosity and creativity.[6] Practices such as meditation and mindfulness also emphasize benefits of clearing the mind, as opposed to staying occupied. So upon reflection, it seems natural that we would alternate between states of boredom and more active engagement. But in a culture that emphasizes keeping busy, our natural tendency is to avoid boredom.

While we might allow for more boring moments, prolonged boredom may still become an issue in retirement. However, rather than repeating the simple advice to 'keep busy', this section focuses on how boredom may be linked to how we structure our time.

How does unstructured free time contribute to boredom?

We are bound by schedules and routines for most of our adult lives. These can become monotonous and 'boring,' or stressful and overly demanding. However, they also motivate us to take action – they create deadlines for the things we need or want to do. Without some of this structured time, retirees often experience a lack of motivation, taking the mindset that things on their to-do list can be done later. Without some timeframe to their plans, retirees find it difficult to follow through with the things they planned and hoped to do in retirement. While they embrace day-to-day freedom, time may seem to slip away – as Iris found, at the beginning of this chapter. Even those that are normally quite curious, creative, and active have struggled with this change in retirement. So it is not necessarily just about your personal characteristics or motivation, but also your environment.

**Tactics to overcome boredom:
Bringing it all together**

1. Allow your curiosity and creativity to flourish.

As we saw, boredom may actually have the benefit of enhancing future curiosity and creativity. These may also be used as an antidote to prolonged boredom, as they involve exploration and generation of new ideas – perhaps ideas of new and engaging pursuits. Getting into a creative mindset is not always so straightforward. One tactic that helps is to identify environments that support a creative, curious mindset. For instance, you may find you are more creative when alone in a quiet place, with a cup of coffee. Or you may be more effective brainstorming with a friend.

Once you get into a creative mindset, take the opportunity to explore opportunities and things you might want to pursue in retirement. In order to foster creativity, disregard worries about obstacles or things that may not work; instead, focus simply on coming up with a range of possibilities and you can home-in on the most interesting or realistic ones later.

Beyond brainstorming ideas for retirement, the practice of fostering curiosity and creativity may be a regular antidote to boredom, allowing you to explore particular hobbies and interests.

2. Identify meaningful and engaging activities.

The ability to choose from several engaging and meaningful activities is another antidote to boredom. As discussed in the chapter *What You Do,* engaging activities are those that are positive, inspiring, important, and challenging. Involvement in these types of activities will keep feelings of boredom at bay, without actually filling your entire day with things to do. For more on this, revisit the chapter *What You Do.*

3. Free time management.

The next antidote to boredom is to actually take action with these intended activities. As mentioned earlier in this chapter, you are most likely to take action by managing your free time—specifically, developing new routines and setting personal goals. This way, your general intentions are transformed to concrete plans with a set timeframe.

THE BUSY RETIREMENT

Many retirees find that they are actually busier in retirement than while they were working. Some consider this a successful retirement. How does this happen? And does such a busy retirement equate to a happy retirement?

Involvement in more activities has been linked to greater satisfaction with retirement.[7] However, researchers have also started exploring the importance of engaging activities in retirement, finding that this is also strongly linked to adjustment and satisfaction.[8] As mentioned in the chapter *What You Do*, engaging activities generally refers to those activities that are experienced as positive, meaningful, and challenging. One study in particular found that participation in such activities was linked to greater wellbeing when compared to participation in activities that were not engaging.[9] In summary, this research suggests that filling your time in retirement is less important than finding a few activities that you find meaningful, positive, and inspiring.

If you find you are quite busy in retirement, you might want to consider the reasons why. Are you constantly being asked to do things? Or do you feel you need to be busy? Or, are you simply taking things at a slower pace and therefore activities are taking up more of the day? Below are a few common reasons retirees find themselves so busy in retirement:

1. "You're retired; you have time...

Others tend to assume that if you're retired, you have the time, availability, and willingness to commit to various other things. As a result, many people find themselves inundated with requests from family, friends, and the community after they retire. These retirees often advise others who are approaching retirement to 'learn to say no' and set some clear boundaries.

2. The work ethic, continued.

"What do people do with a work ethic when they no longer work?" This was the question David Ekerdt asked when he described the busy ethic in retirement.[10] The busy ethic, he explains, is when retirees focus on being active and engaged but have less concern for what they are actually doing to stay busy. As a result, they often fill their days to the brim.

Ekerdt suggests that the busy ethic supports adjustment for those that value an active lifestyle. However, it also appears to continue a cultural emphasis on work and productivity, over rest and leisure. As an alternative, we could focus on the quality of our involvements over quantity, as well as the value of leisure and downtime. Some retirees find they have to learn to allow themselves to slowdown and relax, to enjoy and embrace the personal focus.

3. Things are taken at a slower pace, and simply take longer to do than before.

This may sound like a bit of an oxymoron, but taking things at a slower pace may actually result in fuller days, as your daily tasks simply take longer. A trip to the supermarket, for instance, may be more of the focus for an afternoon without any real rush. Before retirement, it might have been a quick stop on the way home from work. Additionally, health issues may also require taking things at a slower pace.

Most of us need deadlines and time limits to help move things along, so you could choose to create more of a structured plan for the day in order to speed some things up and leave time for other things you'd rather be doing.

If you find you are busier than you would like to be in retirement, try to evaluate the things you are doing and identify those you would like to continue versus those that you're less interested in. Consider how you might set goals and boundaries for your free time, in order to continue only those things you are really interested in.

BRINGING IT ALL TOGETHER

With increased life expectancy, our post-working lives are now representing a significant portion of our lives—those retiring at 65 can expect the next chapter of their lives to last 20 years or more.[1] With much of our lives focused on paid employment, relatively little attention is given to the transition *out* of our careers. What will this new phase of life look like? What will bring fulfillment in this next chapter?

The thought of leaving behind a rewarding career and entering this new chapter in life may be daunting. For others, it's an exciting new adventure. Either way, it is likely to involve some personal adjustments in day-to-day life.

Like any other life transition, retirement is more of a process than an event. It's a period of adjustment that may involve some mixed emotions, some ups and downs, and some trial and error, before settling in to a new lifestyle. Simply put, retirement is not always as easy as we assume, but it may also be a very satisfying and fulfilling time of life.

In the first part of this book you reflected on the story of your career and also your vision for retirement. This represents the beginning of the transition. Whether you are contemplating retirement or are already retired, this is the launch pad for adjusting to, and designing, the next chapter in your life. By reflecting on your career, you may have found some things that you will be letting go of as part of your retirement, and other things that will carry on in some form.

Your visions for an ideal retirement also set the tone for what lies ahead. What is important to you may well be different from what is important to others. It's a good idea to reflect on what retirement means to *you*, personally. However, as you gather new information on retirement, via this book or through conversations with others that have been through the transition, you may clarify a vision for your own retirement. Often times, people are plagued with unnecessary concerns and negative assumptions about retirement; alternatively, some people are surprised by unanticipated changes in retirement. By clarifying realistic expectations, you'll be setting the stage for a smooth transition.

In terms of designing a satisfying new lifestyle in retirement, this book covered four important aspects of retirement, as summarized below: who you are, what you do, who is involved, and how you structure it.

Reflect on your personal traits, preferences, and interests.

A satisfying retirement lifestyle will be rooted in who you are as an individual—your personal values and priorities, interests, and other personal characteristics. The things that are important and interesting to you as you transition, may serve as a compass for how to spend the first part of retirement. Of course, you may also find that this changes over time; you may prefer to mix things up after a few years in retirement.

Because work is often part of how we see ourselves, and how others see us, retirement may also involve some shifts in identity—from seeing yourself according to the work that you do, to seeing yourself according to roles and personal traits that extend beyond the workplace. As other retirees have done, you may find ways of continuing the aspects of work that you connect with most, perhaps even applying your skills and knowledge in new ways. Or, you may find that retirement is an opportunity to shift your focus to other important aspects of your life.

Identify a few engaging - meaningful, challenging, and impactful – activities.

Will your day-to-day activities be fulfilling in retirement? Will you suffer from inactivity or get bored? Those approaching retirement are often advised to keep busy. Researchers are finding, however, that involvement in engaging activities is associated with greater satisfaction and wellbeing.[2] This includes activities that are experienced as positive and inspiring, meaningful and important, impactful, or challenging and requiring commitment. These may range from physical activities to intellectual, social, or even spiritual activities. You may find you are already involved in such activities outside of work; or, you might try out new activities that align with your personal interests, values, or strengths.

Develop and maintain your social network outside of work.

Our relationships and social connections are also a critical part of wellbeing, and researchers are now discovering the important role they play even in our physical and mental health.[3] Because work is often a primary source of social interaction, this is a critical part of retirement. Interactions at work may also be quite positive and supportive; as we often develop close bonds with those we work with. Developing or maintaining relationships outside of the workplace therefore becomes a vitally important part of the retirement transition. Additionally, retirees find that this is something that requires some time and effort—people do not just show up knocking on your door! So it's important to make a point to get out and involved in social activities, even if you're someone that enjoys a bit of solitude.

Communicate openly and prepare for adjustments with your spouse.

Retirement does not happen in a vacuum; it is impacted by, and has an impact on, our family and close relationships. Couples, in particular, face unique adjustments. From increased time together, sharing space around the house, and negotiating household responsibilities, retirement is an entirely new chapter for most couples. An important part of navigating these changes is to maintain open communication throughout the retirement transition. This begins in the pre-retirement phase, discussing retirement plans and expectations. Surprisingly, many couples fail to discuss their plans, as they simply assume that their partner is on the same page.

**Develop a new routine or way
of structuring your time.**

Lastly, work schedules typically take us to one extreme with demanding schedules and not enough free time. But many retirees find an abundance of free time to be problematic as well, leading to reduced motivation and lacking a sense of purpose for the day. Even those that are typically quite active, and have many plans for retirement, will find time simply slipping away without some sort of structure to the days. Developing a new routine and managing one's free time has therefore been found to be an important part of retirement adjustment and satisfaction. This might include committing to regular activities, or setting goals for your free time. Interestingly, retirees with the opposite problem, feeling overwhelmed with too many requests from others, also find that time management is important for dealing with such requests and maintaining time for oneself.

REFLECTIVE QUESTIONS

What is your general vision for retirement? How, if it all, has your vision changed as you reflected on various aspects of retirement (personal values and identity, relationships, engaging activities, and the organisation of time)? Has it become clearer, or raised more questions to consider?

ADDITIONAL TOPICS AND RESOURCES

A WORKING RETIREMENT

The line between work and retirement is blurring, as more people are choosing a 'working retirement' both for financial and personal reasons. In a recent survey by Transamerica, 52% of baby boomers in the US planned to work after retirement.[1] Of those, 62% cited financial reasons while 34% enjoyed work and wanted to stay involved.

That being said, the work people are seeking in retirement is usually different from preretirement. Specifically, most people are looking to continue meaningful work while also transitioning to a more flexible, balanced lifestyle.[2] In other words, they want to continue work in which they have greater control over both their time and the type of work they are involved in.

Working in retirement might mean continuing your pre-retirement work on a more flexible basis. Or, it might mean transitioning to a new job or even a new career. Either way, the following resources may be helpful if you are also considering a working retirement:

Encore.org

Encore.org provides programs to support people who are pursuing a second career with a positive impact on society.

www.encore.org

The Transition Network

The Transition Network is a national organization in the US for women over 50 in transition.

https://www.transitionnetwork.org/

No Desire to Retire

No Desire to Retire is a free website dedicated to over-fifties employment in the UK.

http://www.nodesiretoretire.com/

Greydient

Greydient was recently launched to provide a digital community and recruitment platform for talented older workers and age-friendly employers who value experience over age.

http://www.greydientjobs.com/

VOLUNTEERING

Volunteering is much like paid work, in that it is fairly structured, requiring commitment, time, energy, and oftentimes, working with others. Of course, it is usually more flexible than paid work. Because of this, it can be a great way to meet new people, have an impact, do something meaningful, or utilize your skills and experience in retirement.

The opportunities for volunteer work are endless - whether you want to travel abroad, volunteer in a local community, or even volunteer online. Below are websites where you can search for volunteer opportunities; however, you may also want to visit your local volunteer or community center.

Do-it.org

Do-it.org is the UK's national volunteering database, making it easy for anyone to volunteer in his or her community.

ww.do-it.org

VolunteerMatch

VolunteerMatch provides an online database of volunteer positions, mostly in the US but also in other countries.

www.volunteermatch.org

LIFELONG LEARNING

Lifelong learning has become a bit of a buzzword to describe learning for older adults. Essentially, it refers to learning across the lifespan. We naturally engage in learning well beyond traditional schooling, both through formal and informal outlets, including learning through life experiences. However, the workplace is often an outlet for continuous learning, whether it involves solving new problems, learning new skills, or refining existing skills. Therefore, there may be a tendency for decreased learning once you exit the work environment. One study found that only 50% of retirees were participating in learning, compared to 80% of people still working.[3]

On the other hand, with some goal setting and conscious effort, retirement may also provide increased opportunity for learning, particularly in new areas. It offers the time and freedom to learn about new topics of personal interest, rather than what's needed or required.

What are the benefits of lifelong learning?
There are several benefits to lifelong learning, including enhanced wellbeing, social engagement, personal enrichment, and brain health:

- **Happiness and wellbeing:** Lifelong learning is associated with enjoyment and satisfaction in life, confidence, and the ability to cope. Although health issues and disability can make learning more difficult, research shows that learning may be particularly beneficial for those coping with health problems.[3]

- **Social engagement:** Lifelong learning often leads to increased involvement in social, community, and/or voluntary activities, as well as involvement with younger generations.[3]

- **Personal enrichment:** Most adults are involved in learning for purposes of personal enrichment. Such enrichment may include a sense of achievement, pursuing personal interests, fulfillment, enjoying the challenge of learning and of course, gaining skills, knowledge, and qualifications.[3]

- **Brain health:** Research in neuroscience reveals that the adult brain is really quite 'plastic'.[4] New experiences contribute to the development of new neural pathways and the repair of old cells throughout adulthood. Furthermore, studies have shown that:

Engagement in activities of an intellectual and social nature is associated with slower cognitive decline in healthy older adults . . . Activities that involve effort and challenge contribute to re-sculpting and strengthening neural networks.

Bissland, 2011, p. 13[5]

So, whether you challenge yourself in new ways through hobbies or work, or attend formal classes, it's worth considering some ways in which you might continue your learning.

Forms of Lifelong Learning

Lifelong learning refers to both formal and informal learning, so there are numerous potential outlets. The most common of these might include paid or unpaid work, or college courses. Not all forms of work will provide opportunities for learning; however, many opportunities will provide some challenge and require new skills. More formal learning may also be available through courses at a local university or adult learning classes in the community. Additionally, there are numerous websites now offering free courses online (see below). The only downside is that these usually do not offer the same types of interaction that traditional classroom settings may.

edX
This website offers free online courses from universities, such as Harvard, MIT, Cornell, and Berkeley.
www.edx.org

Coursera
Coursera also offers free courses from universities around the world and in various languages.
www.coursera.org

Future Learn
Future Learn offers free courses from universities and cultural institutions around the world.
www.futurelearn.com

KhanAcademy
This website was started by Salman Khan with the goal to provide "a free world-class education for anyone anywhere." It offers free lectures on math,

science, economics, finance, history, and other topics.
www.khanacademy.org

Udemy

This website offers courses on a wide variety of topics.
Individuals and professionals post their own courses,
with some paid and some free courses.
www.udemy.com

BIBLIOGRAPHY

ABOUT THE BOOK

[1]Braithwaite, V.A., Gibson, D.M. & Bosly-Craft, R. (1986). An exploratory study of poor adjustment styles among retirees. *Social Science & Medicine.* 23(5): 493-499.

Bossé, R., Aldwin, C. M., Levenson, M. R., & Workman-Daniels, K. (1991). How stressful is retirement? Findings from the Normative Aging Study. *Journal of Gerontology, 46*(1), 9-P14.

Szinovacz, M. E. (2003). Contexts and pathways: Retirement as institution, process, and experience. In G. A. Adams & T. A. Beehr (Eds.), *Retirement: Reasons, Processes, and Results* (pp. 6–52). New York: Springer.

Wang, M. (2007). Profiling retirees in the retirement transition and adjustment process: Examining the longitudinal change patterns of retirees' psychological well-being. *Journal of Applied Psychology, 92*(2), 455-474. https://doi.org/10.1037/0021-9010.92.2.455

[2]Steffens, N. K., Cruwys, T., Haslam, C., Jetten, J., & Haslam, S. A. (2016). Social group memberships in retirement are associated with reduced risk of premature death: Evidence from a longitudinal cohort study. *BMJ Open, 6* (2)

PATHWAYS TO RETIREMENT: CASE STUDIES

[1]Csikszentmihalyi, M. (2008). *Flow: The psychology of optimal experience.* New York, NY: Harper Perennial Modern Classics.

INTRODUCTION

[1]Transamerica Center for Retirement Studies. (2016). *The current state of retirement: A compendium of findings about American retirees.* Retrieved from https://www.transamericacenter.org/docs/default-source/retirees-survey/tcrs2016_sr_retiree_compendium.pdf

[2]Hodkinson, P., Ford, G., Hodkinson, H., & Hawthorn, R.

(2008). Retirement as a learning process. *Educational Gerontology*, *34*(3), 167-184.

[3]OECD (2016). Life expectancy at 65 (indicator). https://doi.org/10.1787/0e9a3f00-en

OECD (2016), "Health status", *OECD Health Statistics* (database). http://dx.doi.org/10.1787/data-00540-en

Lee, C. (2001). The expected length of male retirement in the United States, 1850–1990. *Journal of Population Economics, 14*(4), 641–650.

[4]Braithwaite, V.A., Gibson, D.M. & Bosly-Craft, R. (1986). An exploratory study of poor adjustment styles among retirees. *Social Science & Medicine, 23*(5), 493-499.

Bossé, R., Aldwin, C. M., Levenson, M. R., & Workman-Daniels, K. (1991). How stressful is retirement? Findings from the Normative Aging Study. *Journal of Gerontology, 46*(1), 9-14.

Szinovacz, M. E. (2003). Contexts and pathways: Retirement as institution, process, and experience. In G. A. Adams & T. A. Beehr (Eds.), *Retirement: Reasons, Processes, and Results* (pp. 6–52). New York: Springer.

Wang, M. (2007). Profiling retirees in the retirement transition and adjustment process: Examining the longitudinal change patterns of retirees' psychological well-being. *Journal of Applied Psychology,*

92(2), 455-474. https://doi.org/10.1037/0021-9010.92.2.455

[5]Social Security Administration. *Otto von Bismarck.* Retrieved from https://www.ssa.gov/history/ottob.html

[6]Dychtwald, K., Erickson, T. J., & Morison, B. (March 2004). *It's time to retire retirement.* Harvard Business Review. Retrieved from https://hbr.org/2004/03/its-time-to-retire-retirement

[7]Office for National Statistics. (March 2015). *Participation rates in the UK 2014 – 3. Older people.* Retrieved from https://www.ons.gov.uk/employmentandlabourmarket/peopleinwork/employmentandemployeetypes/compendium/participationratesintheuklabourmarket/2015-03-19/participationratesintheuk20143olderpeople

Transamerica Center for Retirement Studies. (2016). *The current state of retirement: A compendium of findings about American retirees.* Retrieved from https://www.transamericacenter.org/docs/default-source/retirees-survey/tcrs2016_sr_retiree_compendium.pdf

[8]Kojola, E. & Moen, P. (2016). No more lock-step retirement: Boomers' shifting meanings of work and retirement. *Journal of Aging Studies, 36*, 59-70. https://doi.org/10.1016/j.jaging.2015.12.003

[9]van Solinge, H. & Henkens, K. (2008). Adjustment to and satisfaction with retirement: Two of a kind? *Psychology and Aging, 23*(2), 422-434. https://doi.org/10.1037/0882-7974.23.2.422

Wang, M., Henkens, K., & van Solinge, H. (2011). Retirement adjustment: A review of theoretical and empirical advancements. *American Psychologist, 66*(3), 204-213. https://doi.org/10.1037/a0022414

[10]Moen, P. (1996). A life course perspective on retirement, gender, and well-being. *Journal of Occupational Health Psychology, 1*(2), 131-144. http://dx.doi.org/10.1037/1076-8998.1.2.131

Kim, J. E., & Moen, P. (2002). Retirement transitions, gender, and psychological well-being a life-course, ecological model. *The Journals of Gerontology Series B: Psychological Sciences and Social Sciences, 57*(3), 212-222. https://doi.org/10.1093/geronb/57.3.P212

Wang, M. (2007). Profiling retirees in the retirement transition and adjustment process: Examining the longitudinal change patterns of retirees' psychological well-being. *Journal of Applied Psychology, 92*(2), 455-474. https://doi.org/10.1037/0021-9010.92.2.455

Wang, M., Henkens, K., & van Solinge, H. (2011). Retirement adjustment: A review of theoretical and empirical advancements. *American Psychologist, 66*(3), 204-213. https://doi.org/10.1037/a0022414

Wang, M. & Shultz, K. S. (2010). Employee retirement: A review and recommendations for future investigation. *Journal of Management, 36*(1), 172-206. https://doi.org/10.1177/0149206309347957

[11]Pinquart, M. & Schindler, I. (2007). Changes of life satisfaction in the transition to retirement: A latent-class approach. *Psychology and Aging, 22*(3), 442-455. https://doi.org/10.1037/0882-7974.22.3.442

Wang, M. (2007). Profiling retirees in the retirement transition and adjustment process: Examining the longitudinal change patterns of retirees' psychological well-being. *Journal of Applied Psychology, 92*(2), 455-474. https://doi.org/10.1037/0021-9010.92.2.455

[12]van der Heide, I., van Rijn, R., Robroek, S., Burdorf, A., & Proper, K. (2013). Is retirement good for your health? A systematic review of longitudinal studies. *BMC Public Health, 13*(1). https://doi.org/10.1186/1471-2458-13-1180

Fabrizio, M., & Franco, P. (2017). Unhealthy Retirement? *Journal of Human Resources, 52*(1), 128-151.

Calvo, E., Sarkisian, N., & Tamborini, C. (2012). Causal effects of retirement timing on subjective physical and emotional health. *The Journals of Gerontology Series B: Psychological Sciences and Social Sciences, 68*(1), 73-84. https://doi.org/10.1093/geronb/gbs097

Behncke, S. (2011). Does retirement trigger ill health? *Health Economics, 21*(3), 282-300. https://doi.org/10.1002/hec.1712

[13]Eibich, P. (2015). Understanding the effect of retirement on health: Mechanisms and heterogeneity. *Journal of Health Economics, 43*, 1-12. http://dx.doi.org/10.1016/j.jhealeco.2015.05.001

Zhu, R. (2016). Retirement and its consequences for women's health in Australia. *Social Science & Medicine, 163*, 117-125. https://doi.org/10.1016/j.socscimed.2016.04.003

Horner, E., & Cullen, M. (2016). The impact of retirement on health: Quasi-experimental methods using administrative data. *BMC Health Services Research, 16*(1). https://doi.org/10.1186/s12913-016-1318-5

Coe, N. B. & Zamarro, G. (2011). Retirement effects on health in Europe. *Journal of Health Economics, 30*(1), 77-86. https://doi.org/10.1016/j.jhealeco.2010.11.002

[14]Clarke, L., & Griffin, M. (2008). Visible and invisible ageing: Beauty work as a response to ageism. *Ageing & Society, 28*(05), 653-674. https://doi.

org/10.1017/s0144686x07007003

[15]Levy, B. (2003). Mind matters: Cognitive and physical effects of aging self-stereotypes. *The Journals of Gerontology: Series B, 58*(4), 203-P211. https://doi.org/10.1093/geronb/58.4.p203

[16]Ng, R., Allore, H., Monin, J., & Levy, B. (2016). Retirement as meaningful: Positive retirement stereotypes associated with longevity. *Journal of Social Issues, 72*(1), 69-85. https://doi.org/10.1111/josi.121564

[17]Levy, B. R., Slade, M. D., Kunkel, S. R., & Kasl, S. V. (2002). Longevity increased by positive self-perceptions of aging. *Journal of Personality and Social Psychology, 83*(2), 261-270. http://dx.doi.org/10.1037/0022-3514.83.2.261

THE BEGINNING: YOUR CAREER

[1]Bridges, W. (2004). *Transitions: Making sense of life's changes.* Cambridge, MA: Da Capo Press.

YOUR RETIREMENT VISION

[1]Knäuper, B., Roseman, M., Johnson, P.J., & Krantz, L. H. (2009). Using mental imagery to enhance the effectiveness of implementation intentions. *Current Psychology, 28*(3), 181. https://doi.

org/10.1007/s12144-009-9055-0

Schwartz, J. M. & Begley, S. (2002). *The mind and the brain: Neuroplasticity and the power of mental force*. New York, NY: HarperCollins.

RETIREMENT AS A PROCESS

[1]Atchley, R. C. (1976). *The sociology of retirement*. Schenkman Publishing Company.

[2]Shultz, K., Morton, K., & Weckerle, J. (1998). The influence of push and pull factors on voluntary and involuntary early retirees' retirement decision and adjustment. *Journal of Vocational Behavior, 53*(1), 45-57. https://doi.org/10.1006/jvbe.1997.1610

[3]Levy, B. R., Slade, M. D., Kunkel, S. R., & Kasl, S. V. (2002). Longevity increased by positive self-perceptions of aging. *Journal of Personality and Social Psychology, 83*(2), 261-270. http://dx.doi.org/10.1037/0022-3514.83.2.261

Ng, R., Allore, H., Monin, J., & Levy, B. (2016). Retirement as meaningful: Positive retirement stereotypes associated with longevity. *Journal of Social Issues, 72*(1), 69-85. https://doi.org/10.1111/josi.121564

[4]Furnham, A. & Marks, J. (2013). Tolerance of ambiguity: A review of the recent literature. *Psychology, 4*(9), 717-728.

[5]Leahy, R. L. (2005). *The worry cure: Stop worrying and start living.* New York, NY: Harmony Books.

[6]Holley-Moore, G. & Beach, B. (2016). *Drink wise, age well: Alcohol use in the over 50s in the UK.* Retrieved from http://www.drinkwiseagewell.org. uk/wp-content/uploads/2016/01/Drink-Wise-Age-Well-Alcohol-Use-and-the-over-50s-Report-2. pdf

[7]Bridges, W. (2004). *Transitions: Making sense of life's changes.* Cambridge, MA: Da Capo Press.

Goins, J. (2013). *The in-between: Embracing the tension between now and the next big thing.* Chicago, IL: Moody Publishers.

[8]Diener, E. & Biswas-Diener (2002). Will money increase subjective well-being? A literature review and guide to needed research. *Social Indicators Research, 57*(2), 119-169.

Kahneman, D., Krueger, A. B., Schkade, D., Schwarz, N., & Stone, A. A. (2006). Would you be happier if you were richer? A focusing illusion. *Science, 312*, 1908 – 1910.

[9]Spano, S. (2017). *The pursuit of time and money: Step into radical abundance and discover the secret to a meaningful prosperous life.* New York, NY: Morgan James Publishing.

[10]Klontz, B. & Klontz, T. (2009). *Mind over money: Overcoming the money disorders that threaten our*

financial health. New York, NY: Crown Publishing Group.

[11]Reitzes, D. C. & Mutran, E. J. (2004). The transition to retirement: Stages and factors that influence retirement adjustment. *The International Journal of Aging and Human Development, 59 (1).*

Taylor, M. A., Goldberg, C., Shore, L. M., & Lipka, P. (2008). The effects of retirement expectations and social support on post-retirement adjustment: A longitudinal analysis. *Journal of Managerial Psychology, 23*(4), 458-470.

Wang, M. (2007). Profiling retirees in the retirement transition and adjustment process: Examining the longitudinal change patterns of retirees' psychological well-being. *Journal of Applied Psychology, 92*(2), 455-474.

[12]Eibich, P. (2015). Understanding the effect of retirement on health: Mechanisms and heterogeneity. *Journal of Health Economics, 43*, 1-12. http://dx.doi.org/10.1016/j.jhealeco.2015.05.001

Zhu, R. (2016). Retirement and its consequences for women's health in Australia. *Social Science & Medicine, 163*, 117-125. https://doi.org/10.1016/j.socscimed.2016.04.003

Horner, E., & Cullen, M. (2016). The impact of retirement on health: Quasi-experimental methods using administrative data. *BMC Health Services*

Research, 16(1). https://doi.org/10.1186/s12913-016-1318-5

Coe, N. B. & Zamarro, G. (2011). Retirement effects on health in Europe. *Journal of Health Economics, 30*(1), 77-86. https://doi.org/10.1016/j.jhealeco.2010.11.002

[13]Atchley, R. C. (1976). *The sociology of retirement.* Schenkman Publishing Company.

MEANING, PURPOSE, AND A MEANINGFUL RETIREMENT

[1]Steger, M. F. (2009). Meaning in life. In S. J. Lopez (Ed.), *Oxford handbook book of positive psychology* (2nd ed.) (pp. 679–687). Oxford: Oxford University Press.

[2]George, L. S., & Park, C. L. (2013). Are meaning and purpose distinct? An examination of correlates and predictors. *The Journal of Positive Psychology, 8*, 365–375.

Heintzelman, S. J., & King, L. A. (2014a). Life is pretty meaningful. *American Psychologist, 69*, 561–574.

Leontiev, D. A. (2013). Personal meaning: A challenge for psychology. *The Journal of Positive Psychology, 8*, 459–470.

[3]Baumeister, R. F., Vohs, K. D., Aaker, J. L., & Garbinskey, E. N. (2013). Some key differences between a

happy life and a meaningful life. *The Journal of Positive Psychology, 8*(6), 505-516.

Schlegel, R., & Hicks, J. (2011). The true self and psychological health: Emerging evidence and future directions. *Social and Personality Psychology Compass, 5*(12), 989-1003. https://doi.org/10.1111/j.1751-9004.2011.00401.x

[4]George, L. S., & Park, C. L. (2013). Are meaning and purpose distinct? An examination of correlates and predictors. *The Journal of Positive Psychology, 8*, 365–375.

[5]Eakman, A. M. (2013). Relationships between meaningful activity, basic psychological needs, and meaning in life: Test of the meaningful activity and life meaning model. *OTJR: Occupation, Participation and Health*, 33(2), 100-109. https://doi.org/10.3928/15394492-20130222-02

[6]Martela, F & Steger, M. F. (2016). The three meanings of meaning in life: Distinguishing coherence, purpose, and significance. *The Journal of Positive Psychology, 11*(5), 531-545. http://dx.doi.org/10.1080/17439760.2015.1137623

[7]Mcknight, P. E., & Kashdan, T. B. (2009). Purpose in life as a system that creates and sustains health and well-being: An integrative, testable theory. *Review of General Psychology, 13*, 242–251.

[8] Hudson, F. (1999) *The adult years: Mastering the art*

of self-renewal. San Francisco, CA: Jossey-Bass.

[9]Rosso, B. D., Dekas, K. H., & Wrzesniewski, A. (2010). On the meaning of work: A theoretical integration and review. *Research in Organizational Behavior, 30,* 91–127. https://doi.org/10.1016/j.riob.2010.09.001

[10]Chalofsky, N. (2003). An emerging construct for meaningful work. (2017). *Human Resource Development International, 6*(1), 69-83. http://dx.doi.org/10.1080/1367886022000016785

[11]Hackman, J., & Oldham, G. (1976). Motivation through the design of work: Test of a theory. *Organizational Behavior and Human Performance, 16*(2), 250-279. https://doi.org/10.1016/0030-5073(76)90016-7

Hackman, J. R. & Oldham, G. R. (1980). *Work redesign.* Reading, MA: Addison-Wesley.

[12]Clark, K. A. (2012). *Long-term unemployment among the baby boom generation: An exploration of coping strategies and subjective well-being* (Doctoral Dissertation). Retrieved from ProQuest.

[13]Dychtwald, K. & Kadlec, D. J. (2010) *A new purpose: Redefining money, family, work, retirement, and success.* New York, NY: HarperCollins.

[14]Baumeister, R. F., Vohs, K. D., Aaker, J. L., & Garbinskey, E. N. (2013). Some key differences between a happy life and a meaningful life. *The Journal of*

Positive Psychology, 8(6), 505-516.

Reker, G. T., & Woo, L. C. (2011). Personal meaning orientations and psychosocial adaptation in older adults. *SAGE Open, 1*(1).

[15] Fave, D. A., Brdar, I., Wissing, M. P., & Vella-Brodrick, D. A. (2013). Sources and motives for personal meaning in adulthood. *The Journal of Positive Psychology, 8*(6), 517-529.

[16] Pinquart, M. (2002). Creating and maintaining purpose in life in old age: A meta-analysis. *Ageing International, 27*(2), 90-114.

[17] George, L. S., & Park, C. L. (2013). Are meaning and purpose distinct? An examination of correlates and predictors. *The Journal of Positive Psychology, 8*, 365–375.

[18] Leontiev, D. A. (2007). Approaching worldview structure with ultimate meanings technique. *Journal of Humanistic Psychology, 47*, 243–266.

[19] Frankl, V. E. (2004). *Man's search for meaning: The classic tribute to hope from the Holocaust.* Reading, UK: Rider.

WHO YOU ARE

[1] Gini, A. (1998). Work, identity and self: How we are formed by the work we do. *Journal of Business Ethics, 17*(7), p. 708.

[2]Price, C. A. (2003). Professional women's retirement adjustment: The experience of reestablishing order. *Journal of Aging Studies, 17*, 341-345.

Borrero, L., & Kruger, T. M. (2015). The nature and meaning of identity in retired professional women. *Journal of Women & Aging*, *27* (4), 309-329.

Duberley, J., Carmichael, F., & Szmigin, I. (2013). Exploring women's retirement: Continuity, context and career transition. *Gender, Work & Organization, 21*(1), 71-90. https://doi.org/10.1111/gwao.12013

WHAT YOU DO

[1]Barbosa, L., Monteiro, B., & Murta, S. (2016). Retirement adjustment predictors—A systematic review. *Work, Aging and Retirement, 2*(2), 262-280. https://doi.org/10.1093/workar/waw008

Butrica, B. A. & Schaner, S. G. (2005). Satisfaction and engagement in retirement. *Perspectives on Productive Aging, 2*.

Nimrod, G. (2007). Expanding, reducing, concentrating, and diffusing: Post retirement leisure behavior and life satisfaction. *Leisure Sciences: An Interdisciplinary Journal*, 29 (1).

[2]Duffy, R.D., Torrey, C.L., England, J., & Tebbe, E.A.

(2016). Calling in retirement: A mixed methods study. *The Journal of Positive Psychology, 12*(4), 399-414.

Jonsson, H., Josephsson, S., & Kielhofner, G. (2001). Narratives and experience in an occupational transition: A longitudinal study of the retirement process. *American Journal of Occupational Therapy, 55*, 424-432.

Pepin, G. & Deutscher, B. (2011). The lived experience of Australian retirees: 'I'm retired, what do I do now?'. *The British Journal of Occupational Therapy. 74*(9), 419-426.

Pushkar, D., Chaikelson, J., Conway, M., Etezadi, J., Giannopoulus, C., Li, K., & Wrosch, C. (2010). Testing continuity and activity variables as predictors of positive and negative affect in retirement. *The Journals of Gerontology Series B: Psychological Sciences and Social Sciences, 65B*(1), 42-49. https://doi.org/10.1093/geronb/gbp079

[3]James, B., Besen, E., Matz-Costa, C., & Pitt-Catsouphes, M. (2012). *Just do it?...maybe not! Insights on activity in later life from the Life & Times in an Aging Society Study*. Chestnut Hill, MA: Sloan Center on Aging & Work, Boston College.

[4]Jonsson, H., Josephsson, S., & Kielhofner, G. (2001). Narratives and experience in an occupational transition: A longitudinal study of the retirement

process. *American Journal of Occupational Therapy*, 55, 424-432.

Pepin, G. & Deutscher, B. (2011). The lived experience of Australian retirees: 'I'm retired, what do I do now?'. *The British Journal of Occupational Therapy*. *74*(9), 419-426.

Jonsson, H., Borell, L., & Sadlo, G. (2000). Retirement: An occupational transition with consequences for temporality, balance and meaning of occupations. *Journal of Occupational Science, 7(1), 29-37.*

Pettican, A.R. & Prior, S. (2011). Retirement: An occupational transition with consequences for temporality, balance and meaning of occupations. *Journal of Occupational Science, 74(1), 12-19.*

[5]Eakman, A.M. (2007). *A reliability and validity study of the meaningful activity participation assessment* (Doctoral Dissertation). Retrieved from ProQuest.

George, L. S., & Park, C. L. (2013). Are meaning and purpose distinct? An examination of correlates and predictors. *The Journal of Positive Psychology*, 8(5), 365–375.

Reker, G. T., & Woo, L. C. (2011). Personal meaning orientations and psychosocial adaptation in older adults. *SAGE Open, 1*(1).

Ryff, C. D., & Singer, B. H. (2008). Know thyself and become what you are: A eudaimonic approach to psychological well-being. *Journal of Happiness*

Studies, 9(1), 13–39.

[6]Baumeister, R., Vohs, K., Aaker, J., & Garbinsky, E. N. (2013). Some key differences between a happy life and a meaningful life. *Journal of Positive Psychology, 8*(6), 505-516.

Chalofsky, N., & Cavallaro, L. (2013). A good living versus a good life: Meaning, purpose, and HRD. *Advances in Developing Human Resources, 15*(4), 331–340.

[7]Arent, S. M., Landers, D. M., & Etnier, J. L. (2000). The effects of exercise on mood in older adults: A meta-analytic review. *Journal of Aging and Physical Activity*, 8, 407–430.

Bosse, A. L., Sheets, E. S., Lett, H. S., & Blumenthal, J. A. (2002). Exercise and the treatment of clinical depression in adults: Recent findings and future directions. *Sports Med, 32*, 741–760.

Price, C. A., & Balaswamy, S. (2009). Beyond health and wealth: Predictors of women's retirement satisfaction. *The International Journal of Aging & Human Development*, 68, 195–214.

Ross, C. E. & Drentea, P. (1998). Consequences of retirement activities for distress and the sense of personal control. *Journal of Health and Social Behavior, 39*(4), 317-334.

[8]Csikszentmihalyi, M. (2008). *Flow: The psychology of optimal experience*. New York, NY: Harper Peren-

nial Modern Classics.

[9]Kojola, E. & Moen, P. (2016). No more lock-step retirement: Boomers' shifting meanings of work and retirement. *Journal of Aging Studies, 36*, 59-70. https://doi.org/10.1016/j.jaging.2015.12.003

[10]Borrero, L., & Kruger, T. M. (2015). The nature and meaning of identity in retired professional women. *Journal of Women & Aging*, *27*(4), 309-29.

Price, C. A. (2000). Women and retirement: Relinquishing professional identity. *Journal of Aging Studies, 14*(1), 81-101.

Strudsholm, T. (2011). *Effect of retirement transition on women's well-being: A study of academic women* (Master's Thesis). Retrieved from University of Calgary Theses.

[11]Borrero, L., & Kruger, T. M. (2015). The nature and meaning of identity in retired professional women. *Journal of Women & Aging*, *27*(4), 309-29.

Gibson, H., Ashton-Shaeffer, C., Green, J., & Corbin, J. (2002). Leisure and retirement: Women's stories. *Society and Leisure, 25* (2), 257-284.

Price, C. A. (2000). Women and retirement: Relinquishing professional identity. *Journal of Aging Studies, 14*(1), 81-101.

Strudsholm, T. (2011). *Effect of retirement transition on women's well-being: A study of academic women* (Master's Thesis). Retrieved from University of

Calgary Theses.

van Solinge, H. & Henkens, K. (2008). Adjustment to and satisfaction with retirement: Two of a kind? *Psychology and Aging, 23*(2), 422-434.

WHO IS INVOLVED

[1]Seligman, M. E. P. (2011). *Flourish: A visionary new understanding of happiness and well-being.* New York: Free Press.

[2]Adams, R. E., Santo, J. B., & Bukowski, W. M. (2011). The presence of a best friend buffers the effects of negative experiences. *Developmental Psychology, 47*(6), 1786–1791.

Cohen, S., & Wills, T. A. (1985). Stress, social support, and the buffering hypothesis. *Psychological Bulletin, 98*(2), 310–357.

[3]Price, C. A., & Balaswamy, S. (2009). Beyond health and wealth: Predictors of women's retirement satisfaction. *The International Journal of Aging and Human Development, 68*(3), 195-214.

Steffens, N. K., Cruwys, T., Haslam, C., Jetten, J., & Haslam, S. A. (2016). Social group memberships in retirement are associated with reduced risk of premature death: Evidence from a longitudinal cohort study. *BMJ Open, 6* (2).

Wang, M., Henkens, K., & van Solinge, H. (2011).

Retirement adjustment: A review of theoretical and empirical advancements. *American Psychologist, 66*(3), 204-213. https://doi.org/10.1037/a0022414

[4]Moen, P., Fields, V., Quick, H., & Hofmeister, H. (2000). A life-course approach to retirement and social integration. In K. Pillemer, P. Moen, E. Wethington, & N. Glasgow (Eds.), *Social integration in the second half of life*. Baltimore: Johns Hopkins University Press.

[5]Jonsson, H., Josephsson, S., & Kielhofner, G. (2001). Narratives and experience in an occupational transition: A longitudinal study of the retirement process. *American Journal of Occupational Therapy, 55*(4), 424-432. https://doi.org/10.5014/ajot.55.4.424

Mein, G., Higgs, P., Ferry, J., & Stansfeld, S. A. (1998). Paradigms of retirement: The importance of health and ageing in the whitehall II study. *Social Science and Medicine, 47* (4), 535-545.

Pepin, G. & Deutscher, B. (2011). The lived experience of Australian retirees: 'I'm retired, what do I do now?'. *The British Journal of Occupational Therapy. 74*(9), 419-426.

Price, C. A. (2002). Retirement for women: The impact of employment. *Journal of Women & Aging, 14*(3-4), 41-57.

[6]Steffens, N. K., Cruwys, T., Haslam, C., Jetten, J., & Haslam, S. A. (2016). Social group memberships in retirement are associated with reduced risk of premature death: Evidence from a longitudinal cohort study. *BMJ Open, 6* (2).

[7]Price, C. A., & Balaswamy, S. (2009). Beyond health and wealth: Predictors of women's retirement satisfaction. *The International Journal of Aging and Human Development, 68*(3), 195-214.

Steffens, N. K., Cruwys, T., Haslam, C., Jetten, J., & Haslam, S. A. (2016). Social group memberships in retirement are associated with reduced risk of premature death: Evidence from a longitudinal cohort study. *BMJ Open, 6* (2)

Wang, M., Henkens, K., & van Solinge, H. (2011). Retirement adjustment: A review of theoretical and empirical advancements. *American Psychologist, 66*(3), 204-213. https://doi.org/10.1037/a0022414

[8]Jung, C. G. (1921) *Psychologische Typen*, Rascher Verlag, Zurich – translation H.G. Baynes, 1923.

[9]Price, C. A. (2002). Retirement for women: The impact of employment. *Journal of Women & Aging, 14*(3-4), 41-57.

[10]Szinovacz, M. E., Ekerdt, D. J., & Vinick, B. H. (Eds.). (1992). *Families and Retirement*. SAGE Publications Inc.

[11]van Solinge, H., & Henkens, K. (2005). Couples' adjustment to retirement: A multi-actor panel study. *The Journals of Gerontology Series B: Psychological Sciences And Social Sciences, 60*(1), S11-S20. https://doi.org/10.1093/geronb/60.1.s11

[12]Griggs, J., Tan, J., Buchanan, A., Attar-Schwartz, S., & Flouri, E. (2009). 'They've always been there for me': Grandparental involvement and child well-being. *Children & Society, 24*(3), 200-214. https://doi.org/10.1111/j.1099-0860.2009.00215.x

Moorman, S., & Stokes, J. (2014). Solidarity in the grandparent–adult grandchild relationship and trajectories of depressive symptoms. *The Gerontologist, 56*(3), 408-420. https://doi.org/10.1093/geront/gnu056

Yorgason, J. B. & Gustafson, K. B. (2014) Linking grandparent involvement with the development of prosocial behavior in adolescents. In Padilla-Walker, L. M. & Carlo, G., *Prosocial development: A multidimensional approach* (201-217). New York, NY: Oxford University Press.

[13]Fidelity Investments (2015). *2015 couples retirement study fact sheet: Disconnects on retirement expectations, social security and income.* Retrieved from https://www.fidelity.com/bin-public/060_www_fidelity_com/documents/couples-retirement-fact-sheet.pdf

[14]Barnes, H., & Parry, J. (2004). Renegotiating identity and relationships: Men and women's adjustments to retirement. *Ageing and Society, 24*(02), 213-233. https://doi.org/10.1017/S0144686X0300148X

Hewitt, A., Howie, L., & Feldman, S. (2010). Retirement: What will you do? A narrative inquiry of occupation-based planning for retirement: Implications for practice. *Australian Occupational Therapy Journal, 57*(1), 8-16. https://doi.org/10.1111/j.1440-1630.2009.00820.x

Robinson, O. C., Demetre, J. D., & Corney, R. H. (2011). The variable experiences of becoming retired and seeking retirement guidance: A qualitative thematic analysis. *British Journal of Guidance & Counselling, 39*(3), 239-258. https://doi.org/10.1080/03069885.2011.562484

HOW YOU STRUCTURE IT

[1]Crego, A., Alcover de la Hera, C., & Martínez-Íñigo, D. (2008). The transition process to post-working life and its psychosocial outcomes: A systematic analysis of Spanish early retirees' discourse. *Career Development International, 13*(2), 186-204. https://doi.org/10.1108/13620430810860576

Hewitt, A., Howie, L., & Feldman, S. (2010). Retirement: What will you do? A narrative inquiry of occupation-based planning for retirement: Implications for practice. *Australian Occupational Therapy Journal, 57*(1), 8-16. https://doi.org/10.1111/j.1440-1630.2009.00820.x

Jonsson, H., Borell, L., & Sadlo, G. (2000). Retirement: An occupational transition with consequences for temporality, balance and meaning of occupations. *Journal of Occupational Science, 7*(1), 29-37. https://doi.org/10.1080/14427591.2000.9686462

[2]Wang, W. C., Wu, C. Y., & Wu, C. C. (2014). Free time management makes better retirement: A case study of retirees' quality of life in Taiwan. *Applied Research Quality Life, 9*(3), 591-604. https://doi.org/10.1007/s11482-013-9256-4

[3]Pepin, G. & Deutscher, B. (2011). The lived experience of Australian retirees: 'I'm retired, what do I do now?' *The British Journal of Occupational Therapy. 74*(9), 419-426. https://doi.org/10.4276/030802211X13153015305556

Pettican, A. & Prior, S. (2011). 'It's a new way of life': An exploration of the occupational transition of retirement. *The British Journal of Occupational Therapy, 74*(1), 12-19. https://doi.org/10.4276/030802211x12947686093521

Price, C. A. (2003a). Professional women's retirement adjustment: The experience of reestablishing order. *Journal of Aging Studies, 17*, 341-345. https://doi.org/10.1016/S0890-4065(03)00026-4

[4]Rubin, R. S. (2002). *Will the real smart goals please stand up?* Retrieved from http://www.siop.org/tip/backissues/tipapr02/03rubin.aspx

[5]Ross, C. E. & Drentea, P. (1998). Consequences of retirement activities for distress and the sense of personal control. *Journal of Health and Social Behavior, 39*(4), 317-334.

[6]Hunter, J., Abraham, E., Hunter, A., Goldberg, L., & Eastwood, J. (2016). Personality and boredom proneness in the prediction of creativity and curiosity. *Thinking Skills and Creativity, 22*, 48-57. https://doi.org/10.1016/j.tsc.2016.08.002

Mann, S. & Cadman, R. (2014). Does being bored make us more creative? *Creativity Research Journal, 26*(2), 165-173. http://dx.doi.org/10.1080/10400419.2014.901073

[7]Nimrod, G. (2007). Expanding, reducing, concentrating and diffusing: Post retirement leisure behavior and life satisfaction. *Leisure Sciences: An Interdisciplinary Journal, 29*(1), 91-111. https://doi.org/10.1080/01490400600983446

Pushkar, D., Chaikelson, J., Conway, M., Etezadi, J., Giannopoulus, C., Li, K., & Wrosch, C. (2010). Testing continuity and activity variables as predictors of positive and negative affect in retirement. *The Journals of Gerontology Series B: Psychological Sciences and Social Sciences, 65B*(1), 42-49. https://doi.org/10.1093/geronb/gbp079

[8]Jonsson, H., Josephsson, S., & Kielhofner, G. (2001). Narratives and experience in an occupational transition: A longitudinal study of the retirement process. *American Journal of Occupational Therapy, 55*(4), 424-432. https://doi.org/10.5014/ajot.55.4.424

Pepin, G. & Deutscher, B. (2011). The lived experience of Australian retirees: 'I'm retired, what do I do now?'. *The British Journal of Occupational Therapy.* 74(9), 419-426. https://doi.org/10.4276/03080 2211X13153015305556

Pettican, A. & Prior, S. (2011). 'It's a new way of life': An exploration of the occupational transition of retirement. *The British Journal of Occupational Therapy, 74*(1), 12-19. https://doi.org/10.4276 /030802211x12947686093521

[9]James, B., Besen, E., Matz-Costa, C., & Pitt-Catsouphes, M. (2012). *Just do it?...maybe not! Insights on activity in later life from the Life & Times in an Aging Society Study*. Chestnut Hill, MA: Sloan Center on Aging & Work, Boston College.

[10]Ekerdt, D. (1986). The busy ethic: Moral continuity between work and retirement. *The Gerontolo-*

gist, 26(3), 239-244. https://doi.org/10.1093/geront/26.3.239

BRINGING IT ALL TOGETHER

[1]OECD (2016). Life expectancy at 65 (indicator). https://doi.org/10.1787/0e9a3f00-en

OECD (2016), "Health status", *OECD Health Statistics* (database). http://dx.doi.org/10.1787/data-00540-en

Lee, C. (2001). The expected length of male retirement in the United States, 1850–1990. *Journal of Population Economics, 14*(4), 641–650.

[2]Jonsson, H., Josephsson, S., & Kielhofner, G. (2001). Narratives and experience in an occupational transition: A longitudinal study of the retirement process. *American Journal of Occupational Therapy, 55*(4), 424-432. https://doi.org/10.5014/ajot.55.4.424

Pepin, G. & Deutscher, B. (2011). The lived experience of Australian retirees: 'I'm retired, what do I do now?'. *The British Journal of Occupational Therapy. 74*(9), 419-426. https://doi.org/10.4276/030802211X13153015305556

Pettican, A. & Prior, S. (2011). 'It's a new way of life': An exploration of the occupational transition of retirement. *The British Journal of Occupational*

Therapy, 74(1), 12-19. https://doi.org/10.4276/030802211x12947686093521

[3]Seligman, M. E. P. (2011). *Flourish: A visionary new understanding of happiness and well-being.* New York: Free Press.

Adams, R. E., Santo, J. B., & Bukowski, W. M. (2011). The presence of a best friend buffers the effects of negative experiences. *Developmental Psychology, 47*(6), 1786–1791.

Cohen, S., & Wills, T. A. (1985). Stress, social support, and the buffering hypothesis. *Psychological Bulletin,* 98(2), 310–357.

ADDITIONAL TOPICS AND RESOURCES

[1]Transamerica Center for Retirement Studies. (2016). *The current state of retirement: A compendium of findings about American retirees.* Retrieved from https://www.transamericacenter.org/docs/default-source/retirees-survey/tcrs2016_sr_retiree_compendium.pdf

[2]Kojola, E. & Moen, P. (2016). No more lock-step retirement: Boomers' shifting meanings of work and retirement. *Journal of Aging Studies, 36,* 59-70. https://doi.org/10.1016/j.jaging.2015.12.003

[3]Dench, S. & Regan, J. (2000). Learning in later life: Motivation and impact. *Institute for Employment*

Studies. Research Brief No 183.

[4]Schwartz, J. M., & Begley, S. (2002). *The mind and the brain: Neuroplasticity and the power of mental force.* New York: Regan Books.

[5]Bissland, V. (2011). *Ways of learning in later life: Older adults' voices* (Dissertation). University of Strathclyde.

ACKNOWLEDGMENTS

I would like to thank all of those who supported and encouraged the development of this book, including my family, friends, colleagues, and the many retirees and pre-retirees who kindly shared their experiences. This book would not have been completed without you.

ABOUT THE AUTHOR

Pauline Johnson-Zielonka, PhD, began exploring the retirement transition in her doctoral research, while interviewing individuals approaching retirement. This is when she realized what a significant life transition this is, and one in which people are generally lacking resources and support. Following her graduate degree, Pauline conducted a review of scientific studies on the challenges and adjustments individuals face in the retirement transition. This research now forms the basis of her current work around retirement transitions.

Pauline's background in industrial-organizational psychology also brings a unique perspective to life planning for retirement and allows her to apply many of the innovative tools and ideas from this field to supporting people transitioning to retirement. Much of her work in I/O psychology involved fitting the right person with the right job in order to enhance both wellbeing and performance. She believes a similar approach may be taken with retirement—helping individuals design a retirement lifestyle that fits their needs and preferences, and enhances their overall wellbeing. Her blend of experience and knowledge in different areas lends a unique, in-depth, and individualised approach to retirement planning.

You can find more information at www.RetirementLifePlan.com

Printed in Great Britain
by Amazon